UNDERSTANDING BLACK MALE
LEARNING STYLES

Jawanza Kunjufu

African American

IMAGES

Chicago, Illinois

CONTENTS

PREFACE: INDIVIDUAL STORIES

Darryl is a brilliant eighth grade rapper. He can listen to a rap CD and in three to five minutes, repeat the words verbatim. Darryl has an auditory learning style. If you don't think this is a skill, try listening to a rap tune for a couple of minutes and then see how many lyrics you can remember.

Despite Darryl's phenomenal skill, he is failing in reading and math. Unfortunately, these two subjects are taught exclusively with textbooks and ditto sheets, two methods that have little effectiveness with Darryl's dominant auditory learning style.

*

Kevin is a super all-around athlete who is currently in the fifth grade. This semester he received an A in physical education, but he failed reading and math. During class he would like to stand up, stretch, and walk around, but his teacher won't let him. She doesn't appreciate that Kevin is a kinesthetic learner who learns best by moving around. Unfortunately, she wants him bolted to his chair like an old desk to the floor.

*

David is a 10th grade student who loves playing video games. When playing his favorite games, he is focused and his concentration is high. A short attention span is never a problem when it comes to playing video games. In fact, he can play one video game for hours at a time. David is the type of young male who can take a gadget apart and put it back together without reading the instructions. Despite David's tremendous intellectual capacity, he is failing in reading and math. What his teacher doesn't know is that he learns best by touching. He is a tactile learner. Unfortunately, in his class, the only thing he is allowed to touch are books and ditto sheets.

*

Willie is a third grade student who spends more time in the corner, outside the door of the classroom, and inside the principal's office than in his classroom. Willie likes working with other students, and he thrives in cooperative learning groups. Last year when the teacher allowed the students to work in pairs and cooperative learning groups, Willie was on the honor roll. This year, the teacher has students working individually. Unfortunately, Willie is failing in reading and math.

INTRODUCTION

I'm a consultant to schools nationwide, and the workshop I'm asked to give most often is "Closing the Racial Academic Achievement Gap." My second most popular workshop is "Understanding Black Male Learning Styles."

This book is a sequel to my national best seller, *Keeping Black Boys Out of Special Education.* In it I asked the question: Is it normal for boys of all races to compromise more than 66 percent of the students who are retained, placed in remedial reading and special education classes, suspended, and who drop out?[1]

When I work with school districts across America, I'm the outsider looking in—and I enjoy being an education consultant. It gives me an objective perspective. I can see things that teachers and administrators can't always see. Or they may know something's wrong, but because they're working with the issue day in and day out, they can't always see how to improve the situation. It helps to have someone come in with a fresh perspective, some who asks questions that, perhaps, they never thought to ask.

When I visit a co-ed school, I expect to see an equal percentage of boys and girls in advanced placement classes, gifted and talented classes, and on the honor roll—as well as in remedial reading and special education classes. I expect to see suspension and dropout rates that are more or less equal. When no such parity exists in the school, this is an urgent red flag for me, and I will immediately begin to ask, "Do you think this is a normal situation?" They already know there's a disparity, but my question helps them to realize that to a certain extent, they've become complacent. Boys will be boys. My challenge is to shake them out of their complacency. No, this situation is not normal. It is unacceptable, and it can no longer go on this way.

Boys of all races are struggling in school. As recently as 2002 there has been a two-to-one ratio of White boys to White girls in special education. During this period, there has been a four-to-one ratio of African American boys to African American girls in special education.[2] Have we designed a female classroom for male students? Are we expecting boys to learn in the same manner as girls?

This book is an attempt to explain the different ways boys, especially African American male students, learn. This book answers the question I am asked most by teachers: "How do we understand Black male learning styles?"

I wrote my books, *Black Students, Middle Class Teachers* and *100+* (and *200+*) *Educational Strategies to Teach Children of Color*, primarily for White female teachers. Eighty-three percent of elementary school teachers in America are White females.[3] Literally, the future of the Black race is in the hands of White female teachers, yet many will admit they did not receive one class on Black history, Black culture, or Black male learning styles in college. They too are laboring under a knowledge gap. This book will inform teachers who are sincere about wanting to understand and help Black males reach their full potential. Further, while this book was written specifically about Black male learning styles, the information also will be helpful in understanding the different ways *all* males learn.

We will discuss in full detail the various theories about learning styles throughout the book, but for now, I'd like to introduce you to the components that comprise the Kunjufu Learning Styles Model:
1. Visual Learners
   a) visual-print
   b) visual-pictures
2. Oral/Auditory Learners
3. Tactile/Kinesthetic Learners

Introduction

If two-thirds of children and an even larger percentage of African American males are right-brain learners (visual-pictures, oral/auditory, tactile/kinesthetic), but 90 percent of the lessons are oriented toward left-brain learners (visual-print), then Houston, we have a problem.[4] The conflict between pedagogy and the dominant learning styles of Black males forms the central problem that we'll seek to resolve in this book.

A significant percentage of African American male students are right-brain learners, and they are struggling every day to learn from teachers who use textbooks and ditto sheets and nothing else. That's like speaking only one language to a group of students who speak English, Swahili, Spanish, Arabic, and French. Quite a few will not understand what's being said—and then they'll be penalized for not understanding!

When I was a classroom teacher, my mentor taught me that you don't teach the way you want to teach. You teach the way your children learn. If two-thirds of your class are right-brain learners, it makes no sense to spend most of your time teaching from textbooks and ditto sheets. You must adjust your pedagogy.

I want to take this time to acknowledge the late Dr. Rita Dunn. She dedicated more than 30 years of her life to understanding learning styles and appealing to teachers to adjust their pedagogy to meet children's learning needs.

One of the more interesting findings to come from her research is that learning styles are *more than 80 percent biologically imposed.*[5] I want to stress the significance of that last statement. What if a left-handed student was forced to use his right hand in the classroom? It's as if many teachers, either intentionally or in a state of denial, want to reject the research that documents the fact that 80 percent of how children learn is biologically imposed. Academic performance is not based on culture. It's not based on poverty. It's not based on the demographics of the home or the educational background of the parents. Learning styles are biologically driven. The fact that we are insisting that right-brain learners only learn from textbooks and ditto sheets is, in my opinion, criminal.

If learning styles are biologically driven, then teachers will have to adjust *their* methods before even thinking about trying to fix the students.

What I love most about Rita Dunn's work is that it was not just theoretical. She provided very clear and practical examples, and I encourage you to read all of her work.

I'd like to close this Introduction with what I believe was Dr. Dunn's greatest contribution to this subject. **When school districts in North Carolina and Louisiana implemented a pedagogy that was congruent with children's learning styles (thus improving teacher quality), Dr. Dunn discovered that in North Carolina, scores rose from the 30th percentile to the 83rd percentile. In Louisiana, scores rose from the 30th percentile to the 78th percentile.**[6] This tremendous improvement in test scores further strengthens my own research base and offers educators evidence that attention to learning styles is a valid approach to closing the racial academic achievement gap.

Dr. Dunn's research inspires me and helps me make a solid case to followers of Ruby Payne, who have convinced themselves that it is the income of the home, the number of parents in the home, the educational background of the parents, and the racial make-up of the children that determine intelligence and academic potential.[7] We could close the racial achievement gap in a school year, in a semester, if we simply changed our pedagogy, curricula, and lesson plans.

In the next chapter, we will quantitatively document the conflict between pedagogy and the dominant learning styles of Black males.

CHAPTER 1: THE PROBLEM

5,000 children are expelled
from preschool annually.
90 percent are male.[1]

*

Only 12 percent of African American
boys are proficient in reading.[2]

*

More than 70 percent of remedial
reading students are male.[3]

*

70 percent of all D's and F's are
earned by males.[4]

*

80 percent of African American students in special education are male.[5]

*

66 percent of the students suspended are male.[6]

*

53 percent of all African American males drop out of high school.[7]

*

Some school districts retain almost 20 percent of their kindergarten students, most of whom are male.[8]

Chapter 1: The Problem

The following is a list of 20 African American third grade males, who took the Iowa Reading Test. This chart shows their performance and that of 20 students chosen at random. Overall, the chart shows how well the students performed over the past five years beginning at the third grade.[9]

Beginning Third Grade Percentile	Ending Seventh Grade Percentile	Reading Progress (Years)
98	35	1.3
97	54	2.7
92	24	2.1
91	68	3.1
81	72	3.9
72	72	3.6
66	59	3.9
63	7	0.7
63	4	0.0
57	39	3.2
47	9	2.1
41	11	2.5
29	12	3.0
21	44	5.6
21	29	4.7
21	17	3.8
18	1	1.3
16	39	4.6
7	30	4.5
5	5	3.2

While these quantitative statistics are enlightening, I believe the most demoralizing problem is qualitative. When I visit schools and see a Black boy in the corner or sitting in the hall while other students are engaged in the lesson, I take it personally, as if the child were my own son or grandson. Later, if I was to ask him, "How was school today?" and he told me that he spent most of the day in the corner or in the hall, I would immediately schedule a meeting with the teacher. This scenario sheds light on how the spirits of our boys are being broken.

When I visit a school to meet with the principal and see Black male students waiting to meet with the disciplinarian, I look at the sullen, listless, and angry expressions of these sons and grandsons with sadness. I already know how school was today. I see the looks in their eyes. Their spirits have been broken.

How many weeks, days, hours, or minutes have Black boys spent in the corner, outside the classroom door, or in the principal's office? How many opportunities to learn have been missed? How many boys' spirits have been broken?

According to Yale University's first nationwide study of expulsion rates in state-supported preschools, the process begins before kindergarten. According to the researchers, "Preschools are expelling youngsters at three times the rate of public schools....boys are being thrown out of preschool 4 1/2 times as frequently as girls. African American preschoolers are twice as likely to be expelled as white or Latino children, and five times as likely as Asian Americans."[10]

Despite this alarming trend, I challenge you to visit a kindergarten class. If you want to see Black boys at their best, look at them in kindergarten. They're eager, they're curious, they're on task. They love learning. Unfortunately, by the ninth grade, they're no longer sitting in the front row. They're no longer on task. They're asleep, bored, and probably are about to drop out. Their spirits have been broken. In the next chapter, we will develop the framework for this book.

CHAPTER 2: FRAMEWORK

In this chapter I will raise the issues that will become more fully developed throughout the book. These issues form the framework, driving force, and foundation of my approach to understanding Black male learning styles and what schools must do to address the learning needs of this neglected population.

- Is there a correlation between the high percentage of White female teachers in public schools and the high percentage of African American males in special education?

- Very few left-brain learners have Attention Deficit Disorder (ADD). Very few visual-print learners have ADD.[1]

- In my opinion and those of others in education and psychology, ADD was invented to justify teachers' expectation of students, including boys, to sit still for long periods of time, work by themselves, and work quietly on boring textbooks and ditto sheets.

- Theoretically we know that students learn differently. We simply do not make the adjustments in our pedagogy, curricula, lesson plans, and classroom management.

- If all children can learn, why aren't they?

- Right-brain students who are taught analytically and sequentially become low achievers.[2]

- Based on patterns of placement if there were only female students, there would be little need for special education.[3]

- If your students are not learning the way you teach, then teach the way they learn.

- *How* you teach is as important as *what* you teach.

- If you want to *train* students, then ask most of the questions—and have predetermined answers. If you want to *educate* students, however, encourage *them* to ask questions, and make sure the questions are open-ended.

- Teach the way your students enjoy learning.

- Master teachers do not see broken children nor do they believe in the cultural deficit model.[4] They build on the culture the students bring to the classroom.

- Pedagogy is more than instructional style. It's the mindset teachers have for their students.

- Your students will be as enthusiastic as you are about the lesson plan.

- Ninety percent of K-12 instruction comes from textbooks and ditto sheets.[5]

- If your classroom has more than 30 students and desks that don't move, this could be a problem.

- We could reduce special education placements if physical education was offered on a daily basis.

- Pedagogy in low-income schools has not changed much in the past 100 years.

- Boys do not have a short attention span if they are involved in something that interests them.

- From kindergarten to 12th grade, students attend school 13,000 hours, yet they only receive two days of individualized attention.[6]

- Are we preparing students to work in factories that no longer exist?

- Asthma, lead paint, bad diet, and being born addicted to crack cocaine do not produce good students.

- "Underachievers" tend to be right-brain learners.[7] So is the problem the way they learn or the way we teach?

- We should encourage students to ask, "Why do we need to learn this?"

- Learning style is 80 percent biologically driven.[8]

- Low literacy achievement in primary grades often leads to aggressive behavior in upper grades.[9]

- The writing gap between genders exceeds the racial and income gap.[10]

- Learning styles are not like clothes that can be added or removed. It's *who* we are.

- Instead of tracking, dividing, or categorizing students by test scores, let's organize students according to their learning styles.

- How can teachers say Black boys cannot learn math or science when they can bounce a ball 30 inches in circumference at 20 miles per hour on a court 94 feet in length and jump 10 feet high from the free throw line, which is 15 feet from the basket, and dunk the ball into a basket 62 inches in circumference?

- In most classrooms, students perform only one task at a time. The reality is that 21st century students are multitaskers. How can you say a student cannot learn when he can listen to his iPod, send text messages, and make comments on Facebook and Twitter all while calling a friend and playing a video game?

- In classrooms that are left-brain oriented, students perform only one task at a time. Right-brain learners are multitaskers.[11]

- We could reduce or perhaps even eliminate the ADD label if we allowed students to multitask.

We like to say that children come first, but as the statistics show, that has not been the case in our schools. In fact, I've seen union members with t-shirts and posters that say "Teachers first." Until we mean what we say and truly put children first, all the books that I and other researchers and educators have written will gather dust in the teachers' lounge.

The research has spoken. The models are sound. So why are our boys still lagging behind? I submit that we haven't yet created learning environments that meet the needs of *all* students, especially African American males.

Presently, the vast majority of our schools are controlled by unions. One reason why parents choose private schools and charter schools is because they do not want their schools controlled by teachers. They want a school environment where they have a say and children come first.

Do you know how difficult it is for a principal to remove an incompetent teacher? On average it will cost a school district $100,000 that they do not have and three to five years to *transfer* a teacher.[12] Note the word *transfer*. Because of strong unions, incompetent teachers are allowed to keep their jobs to the detriment of our children. This is the teacher who was found sleeping in class, who missed more than 20 days of school, who was chronically late, whose lesson plans were not fully developed, who did not check homework, whose student scores did not improve, whose students were caught on videotape sleeping, playing cards, and doing whatever they wanted as long as they did not bother the teacher. This is the teacher who tells her students, "I get paid whether you learn or not." This is the teacher who is often transferred to another low achieving school.

It would take three to five years and another $100,000 that a school does not have to fire a low-performing teacher.[13] If school districts could eliminate the bottom 10 percent of their teachers and use that money to pay for Master Teachers, we could compete against the top rated countries in education. The reality is only one out of 2500 teachers will lose their license in contrast to one of 95 lawyers and one of 57 doctors.[14]

If you've read any of my books, you know the five types of teachers:

- Custodians
- Referral Agents
- Instructors
- Teachers
- Coaches

Custodians have low expectations of their students, poor time on task, poor classroom management skills, and principals have a very difficult time getting them removed.

Referral Agents are quick to recommend students to special education and the principal's office for disciplinary problems.

Instructors believe they teach subjects, not students. Unfortunately, after the primary grades we have an increase of instructors.

Unfortunately, all types of teachers, including Custodians, Referral Agents, and Instructors are protected by tenure agreements and unions, so they don't have to make any changes in their pedagogy. Principals cannot mandate that teachers understand Black male learning styles. They don't have to develop lesson plans conducive for right-brain learners. In nearly every school district in the U.S., there is absolutely no accountability.

On the other hand, **Master Teachers** not only understand their subject matter like Instructors, they also understand the importance of developing a pedagogy that is congruent with their children's learning styles. They understand that *how* you teach is just as important as *what* you teach. If we had more Master Teachers who understood this truism, we would see an improvement in the academic performance of African American males.

Finally, **Coaches** not only understand subject matter like Instructors and congruence of pedagogy and learning styles like Master Teachers, they also understand the children's culture.

In the next chapter we will look at the importance of African American male culture.

CHAPTER 3: BLACK MALE CULTURE

Please take the following quiz.

1. What is culture?

2. What is the cultural deficit model?

3. Are Black boys culturally deprived if they do not possess your culture?

4. Do you like Black boys?

5. What are their strengths?

6. Are you afraid of tall Black boys?

7. Do you like the way they walk?

8. Do you like the way they talk?

9. Do you like their swagger?

10. Do you know why the pants of some boys sag?

11. What are the Dozens?

12. Do you know why some boys play the Dozens?

13. What are the language arts skills needed to play the Dozens?

14. What is the difference between how Black and White cultures view words?

15. Do you know why some Black boys want to be the class clown?

16. Why do some African American males associate being smart with acting White?

17. Why do some African American males associate being smart with femininity?

18. How many boys in your class have fathers who live with them?

19. Describe a mama's boy.

20. What are the classroom implications of educating a mama's boy?

21. How many adult Black males are in your school?

22. How many are classroom teachers?

23. What do you know about the male ego?

24. Do you believe we should teach Black boys as if they were in the military?

25. What happens to the Black boy's spirit when you send him to the corner, outside the door, or to the principal's office?

26. What are the three most popular careers for Black males?

Chapter 3: Black Male Culture

27. What do you think your Black male students will be doing when they're 30 years of age?

28. What is the showdown?

29. What is cool pose?

30. What is *106 & Park*?

31. What are rites of passage?

32. How do your Black male students feel about working together in groups?

33. How do they feel about competition?

34. Why is there a disproportionate number of boys in your school in special education, remedial reading, earning poor grades, suspended, and dropping out?

35. Does sexism exist in your school?

36. What is the worst comment you've heard in the teachers' lounge or cafeteria about Black boys?

In the next section, we will provide answers to some of these questions.

Cultural Deficit Model

The definition of culture is lifestyle. Everyone has a lifestyle, but many Whites and middle-class African Americans believe that if you don't have White middle-class values, you are culturally deprived. Many educators believe that if you do not come from a middle-income home with two parents who are college educated and speak Standard English, then you are culturally deprived. This is the cultural deficit model.

According to the cultural deficit model, the problem is with the student, not with the system or the teachers. So many times schools bring me in to fix the "bad" children. The assumption is that there's nothing wrong with the teachers, curriculum, pedagogy, or administration. The cultural deficit model presumes there is something wrong with Black boys.

Strengths

If African Americans were inferior, there would be no need for racism. African American students have many strengths that have been overlooked by teachers. Those strengths include their unique, clever, witty, creative, sensitive, and strong auditory skills, oral skills, visual-picture skills, and tactile/kinesthetic skills.

Chapter 3: Black Male Culture

Every teacher needs to focus on the strengths of her students, not their deficiencies.

Saggin'

Saggin' has its roots in the American prison system where inmates are prohibited from wearing belts that they could use to hurt themselves or other inmates. As a result, their pants drop down or sag. Some African American males who have a defiant oppositional view of White mainstream America have continued the look outside of prison, and now it's an unfortunate fashion statement. Ironically, some White fashion designers adopted the look for their menswear lines.

By the way, if you look at the word saggin' backwards, it says something else.

The Dozens

The Dozens (crackin', rankin', signifyin') is a verbal word game. In male culture there's a desire to find out who's the best—or in Ebonics, who's the baddest. Since schools have rules against fighting (rightfully so), African American males created a nonviolent way to blow off steam and determine who's the baddest on the playground. The Dozens is a verbal word game that plays off the most valued persons in the Black community, mothers.

Language arts skills are needed to play the Dozens well: making words rhyme, a constantly expanding vocabulary, quick thinking skills, and a comfort with speaking in public.

In White culture, words are taken literally. In Black culture, words are figures of speech. Let's say a teacher is listening to two boys playing the Dozens. Taking their words literally, she assumes, incorrectly, that the boys are about to fight. Actually the boys are trying to *avoid* a fight. If they are allowed to continue, she'll find that they'll be the best of friends minutes later. Interestingly, the loser will probably use the winner's lines in his next Dozens match against another student.

The Class Clown

The class clown acts out because he is trying to cover up his academic deficiencies. It is embarrassing being in eighth grade with low level reading and math skills. One of the ways to avoid the embarrassment is to act like the class clown. This student doesn't care about how the teacher feels about his antics, but getting the respect of his peers, even through laughter, means everything to him.

The class clown hopes that the teacher will put him out of the classroom, but this is the last thing teachers should do. Instead, tell the student in no uncertain terms, "I know exactly what you're trying to do. You want me to put you out, but there's nothing you can do that would provoke me to put you out of my class."

Students who clown around are in desperate need of attention. Unfortunately, most teachers and parents will give more attention to negative behavior than positive behavior.

Since the student thinks he's funny, consider giving him the last couple of minutes of the class period or school day to perform. Those students who are not as funny as they think may refuse and no longer act like the class clown. Students who really are funny may take you up on it, and you may be helping them to launch a career in entertainment. African American comedians Bill Cosby and Richard Pryor were class clowns in their younger years.

In fact, Richard Pryor used comedy as a way to survive his environment.

> "Living in one of the worst slums in Peoria, Illinois, Pryor found that he could best defend himself by getting gang members to laugh at him instead of pummeling him. This led to his reputation as a disruptive class clown, though at least one under-standing teacher allowed Pryor one minute per week to 'cut up' so long as he behaved himself the rest of the time."[1]

Maybe when your students become famous, they'll give you a royalty for giving them a stage and an opportunity to perform.

Being Smart Is Acting White

Of all the beliefs African American male students share, the belief that being smart is acting White creates the most damage to their academic performance and self-esteem. This belief developed over time because schools have not done a good job of teaching African American children their history and culture. For one month out of the year (February, the shortest month), schools teach an incomplete version of Black history that begins in slavery, in 1620, rather than in Egypt or Africa five million years ago.

If students know that Imhotep, not Hippocrates, was the first doctor, they will not associate being smart with acting White. If they know that their ancestors built the pyramids, they will not associate being smart with acting White.

On the other hand, it is possible that teachers and parents are doing their job, but the peer group is discouraging academic achievement by spreading false information. We must do everything in our power to change the minds of our children. One way is by having them research which of their favorite rappers and ballplayers earned their college degrees. We must also expose them to African American males who are earning large salaries outside of sports and entertainment.

Mama's Boy

Some mothers raise their daughters and love their sons. They have double standards for their sons and daughters. They make their daughters come in early and not their sons. They make their daughters study and not their sons. They make their daughters do chores and not their sons. As a result, in many families, the girls are far more responsible than the boys.

Black women are experts on Black men, yet many of them raise trifling, irresponsible sons.

The implications of a mama's boy in the classroom are significant. He feels that you, the teacher, are too hard on him, too demanding, and your expectations are too high. These males are confident that their mothers will come to their defense and appeal to you to be less demanding. It is your responsibility to not only understand the mama's boy syndrome but to maintain high expectations of your students as well.

Ego

The male ego is very large and fragile. Many schools believe the best way to teach Black boys is to break them down and then build them back up as if they were in the military. There's nothing more disheartening than to see a male student whose spirit has been broken. We need to be careful with the male ego. For example, perhaps a male child shouldn't be forced to read aloud if you know he won't do well. If you send a boy to the board to do a math problem, you should feel confident that he will do it well. The goal of education should be to develop students' innate intelligence, not humiliate and berate them in front of their peers.

The Three Most Popular Careers

The three most popular careers for African American males are sports, rap, and drugs. For many boys there's only the NBA and the NFL. They dream of becoming a professional athlete, but they don't realize that earning a spot on a team would be defying the odds; one million males are seeking one of seven full-time jobs that will last on average four years. Unfortunately, they feel more confident pursuing a spot in the NBA than a career in science or math.

The second dream of many boys is to become a rapper. Honing their skills while playing the Dozens and freestyling, some have progressed to the next level and are writing rap lyrics. I've read some of these long-form poems and have been impressed with their creativity and thoughtfulness.

The reality, though, is that few rappers are able to maintain their million dollar lifestyles beyond five years. That leaves selling drugs. Unfortunately, many boys believe it is easier to sell crack than CISCO, Microsoft, and IBM. We need to expand our boys' career horizons.

CLASSROOM EXERCISES

1. Have students name a different career for each letter of the alphabet. That includes q, x, y, and z.

2. Teachers, see if you can identify a famous African American in each career named by the students.

3. Ask your male students what they want to be when they are 30 years old (excluding a professional athlete, rapper, or drug dealer). Find a picture of a famous African American and put that picture next to your students' pictures on the bulletin board.

The Showdown

In the primary grades, teachers use their size to discipline students. In the intermediate and upper grades, boys have grown taller and bigger than their teachers. It is no secret that some teachers are afraid of our boys. It is difficult, if not impossible, to educate a child if you are afraid of him.

The showdown is a power struggle between boys and female teachers. Boys are usually confident that you are afraid of them and that you are going to back down.

There are at least six ways the showdown could play out in the classroom:

Showdown #1: She says unassertively, "Sit down." Well, he may sit down later in the afternoon. Because he knows she's nervous around him, he doesn't respect her, and she can never be effective as his teacher.

Showdown #2: She's inconsistent. She responds to him some of the time but not all the time. Whenever she doesn't respond, he wins the showdown.

Showdown #3: She becomes emotional. Students love it when a White female teacher turns red while she's chasing a student around the classroom. He wins the showdown.

Showdown #4: She says, "I'm going to send you to the only male in the building." He may lose to the male authority, but he wins the showdown with the female teacher.

Showdown #5: She's assertive. The tone of her voice and eye contact says she means business, and the student recognizes that. She wins the showdown.

Showdown #6: She's consistent. She responds to the student the same way each and every time. She wins the showdown.

The good news is that your male students are hoping you'll find a respectful way to check their behavior. Yes, they actually want you to win the showdowns. Role playing these and other scenarios with teachers and administrators will strengthen your communications skills. Both verbal and body language skills are important to master the showdown: tone of voice, consistent discipline, physical posture, eye contact, controlled facial expression, control of emotions, assertiveness. As you master these skills, classroom management will improve as well.

Cool Pose

Cool pose is based on materialism, and as long as students acquire things, then their male peer group, females, and the larger society will deem them as being successful. Many boys would rather hang out on the playground than be involved in structured sports that requires answering to a coach, arriving to practice on time, playing defense, being disciplined, and following the rules. To the contrary, cool pose is about hanging out on the playground or on the corner with no structure, no adult supervision. It allows them to profile their looks, their clothes, their jewelry, their cars, and their possessions. Cool pose is about showing mainstream White America that they can be successful without compromising, acting White, wearing a tie, speaking Standard English, or staying in school.

106 & Park

106 & Park is a popular television show on BET that runs daily, and it features the top 10 music videos of the week. I would strongly recommend that you utilize students' interest in their culture and these videos to teach language arts skills. If I were a classroom teacher, I would devise appropriate ways to incorporate *106 & Park* into my lesson plans.

CLASSROOM EXERCISES

1. Bring in a PG-13 rated version of the number one video featured on *106 & Park*. Play it for the students, which they would truly enjoy, and then have the spelling words for the week come from that video.

2. Have students write about what they saw in the video. Use the lyrics to teach a lesson. For example, one popular video has been *Can't Leave 'Em Alone*, featuring 50 Cent and Ciarra. In the video Ciarra says, "I tried that good boy game, but that dope boy is turning me on." (This is another reason why so many boys assume the cool pose.) The lyrics are clearly saying that this fine looking sister, Ciarra, tried that good boy who was acting White, who was an honor roll student, but he did

not appeal to her. But the drug dealer, the rapper, the ball player, the brother who had cool pose attracted her. We need to engage students in these types of discussions.

106 & Park can launch some great educational moments in your classroom.

Rites of Passage

In traditional societies, men separate boys from the society, and women separate the girls. They define for boys what it means to be a man. When the boys meet that criteria, then there's a ceremony where they are bestowed with the honor of being a man.

Unfortunately, in modern societies, boys and girls are clueless about what it takes to be a man or a woman. Many boys who lack fathers and male mentors have defined manhood based on criteria such as how cool you are, how well you fight, how well you play ball, how many girlfriends you have, and how many babies you've made. In some cities, dropping out of school, killing someone, and going to jail are rites of passage.

Every school should create a rites of passage program that will be taught before, during, or after school. Additional literature on rites of passage programs is included in my earlier books, including *Countering the Conspiracy to Destroy Black Boys*.[2]

Cooperative Learning and Competition

Boys love working together in pairs. They also like working in cooperative learning groups of four to six students. They will become even more engaged if they can compete against a female group. Cooperative learning and competition don't have to be juxtaposed. They complement each other. Using single gender male cooperative learning groups in competition against girls is an excellent way to maximize the potential of African American males. In the next chapter we will look at learning styles.

CHAPTER 4: LEARNING STYLES

One day a class was treated to a guest lecture from a man who had been in a war. As the gentleman was giving his lecture, an oral presentation only, no maps, pictures, or other images, he stood over one of the students who had dutifully chosen a seat front and center. The lecturer noticed that the student was doodling in his notebook. He held the notebook up for the entire class to see and said, "I hope the rest of you are paying more attention than this young man." The student was, of course, horribly embarrassed.

After class, the doodler approached the guest teacher and explained that doodling was how he took notes. He asked the gentleman to quiz him on any of the material. The guest teacher did, and the student was able to answer each question correctly. The student had drawn outlines of countries the gentleman had visited. He had drawn weapons the man had used from the descriptions given, and he had engraved them with the years the man had visited there.

The doodler had remembered all of the new material because he had created pictures of the details, both in his notebook and in his mind. Pictures have permanence.

The guest teacher apologized to the class the next day, saying he did not realize that students could effectively take notes in pictures. For visual learners who excel in thinking in images, notes and other important information are better recalled when they are converted into pictures.[1]

How many doodlers are in your class? How would you have responded if you had seen one of your students doodling while you were giving your lecture?

UNDERSTANDING BLACK MALE LEARNING STYLES

Do you acknowledge that children learn in different ways? Do you have any students in your class who:

- Skip over directions?
- Find it hard to listen to directions?
- Lose attention when someone is talking?
- Like to take action before reading instructions?
- Make careless errors?
- Do not like paper and pencil tasks?
- Like physical movement?
- Like someone to show them how to do something?
- Look around to see if classmates are working before beginning their assignment?
- Look at the pictures in the book before reading?
- Value relationships with students over content?
- Like to draw or doodle?
- Have difficulty sitting still for long periods of time?
- Prefer to multitask?
- Can take an object apart and explain each part's function?
- Daydream?
- Love music and drama?
- Draw well?
- Have short attention spans when bored?
- Can listen to a rap CD and remember every word?
- Can play a video game longer than three hours?

Have you met the needs of the above students?

Chapter 4: Learning Styles

Do the following traits and activities describe the ideal student?

- Quiet
- Can sit still for long periods of time
- Works independently
- Long attention span
- Likes ditto sheets and textbooks
- Left-brain learner
- Passive
- Teacher pleaser
- Raises hand before speaking
- Mastered reading before second grade
- Neat
- Well developed fine motor skills
- Good handwriting
- Well organized
- Likes multiple choice exams
- Likes departmentalization
- Mature
- White
- Female
- Middle class
- Two-parent home
- Mother works from home and possesses a college degree

Does the following describe your most challenging student?

- Loud
- Likes to stand or walk around
- Prefers playing in groups
- Short attention span

- Hates ditto sheets and textbooks
- Right-brain learner
- Aggressive
- Likes to challenge teachers
- Speaks without raising hand
- Slow reader
- Junky
- Poor fine motor skills
- Poor handwriting skills
- Disorganized
- Prefers oral exams
- Prefers one teacher
- Immature
- African American
- Male
- Low income
- Single parent
- Mother works two jobs and is a high school drop-out

Throughout this chapter I will provide my theoretical framework for understanding learning styles. As college students, we learned all about the split brain theory. Two hemispheres of the brain, left and right. Left side, analytical. Right side, holistic. Unfortunately, we did not learn how to incorporate this knowledge into our pedagogy. As you read through the following charts and graphs, think about how your African American male students have responded thus far to your lesson plans and classroom management. Even Master Teachers and Coaches know there is always room for improvement. Hopefully this information should shed light on how you can begin to better meet the learning needs of your students.

Chapter 4: Learning Styles

The following chart by Rosalie Cohen[2] describe the contrasts between left-brain and right-brain thinkers, and between the analytical style and relational style.

Left-Brain Students	Right-Brain Students
As it is in general (Analytical)	As it could be (Relational)
Rules	Freedom
Standardization	Variation
Conformity	Creativity
Memory of specific facts	Memory for essence
Regularity	Novelty
Rigid order	Flexibility
"Normality"	Uniqueness
Differences equal deficits	Sameness equals oppression
Preconceive	Improvise
Precision	Approximate
Logical	Psychological
Atomistic	Global
Egocentric	Sociocentric
Convergent	Divergent
Controlled	Expressive
Meanings are universal	Meanings are contextual
Direct	Indirect
Cognitive	Affective
Linear	Patterned
Mechanical	Humanistic
Unison	Individual in group
Hierarchical	Democratic
Isolation	Integration
Deductive	Inductive
Scheduled	Targets of opportunity

Next, Bernice McCarthy, the creator of the 4Mat System, believes there are four types of learners:[3]
1. Innovative: Teachers need to create a reason for learning. Key question: why?
2. Analytic: Teachers need to give them the facts. Key question: what?
3. Common sense: Teachers need to let them try it. Key question: how?
4. Dynamic: Teachers need to let them teach themselves through discovery. Key question: what if?

The third model comes from Cynthia Tobias.[4]

Four Combinations	
Concrete Sequential (CS)	**Abstract Sequential (AS)**
hardworking conventional accurate stable dependable consistent factual organized	analytic objective knowledgeable thorough structured logical deliberate systematic
Abstract Random (AR)	**Concrete Random (CR)**
sensitive compassionate perceptive imaginative idealistic sentimental spontaneous flexible	quick intuitive curious realistic creative innovative instinctive adventurous

Chapter 4: Learning Styles

The next model comes from Howard Gardner.[9]

Eight Ways of Learning			
Children who are highly . . .	**Think . . .**	**Love . . .**	**Need . . .**
Linguistic	in words	reading, writing, telling stories, playing word games	books, tapes, writing tools
Logical-Mathematical	by reasoning	experimenting, questioning, figuring out logical puzzles, calculating	materials to experiment with, science materials, manipulatives, trips to planetariums and science museums
Spatial	in images and pictures	designing, drawing, visualizing, doodling	art, Legos, videos, movies, slides, imagination games, mazes, puzzles, illustrated books, trips to art museums
Bodily-Kinesthetic	through somatic sensations	dancing, running, jumping, building, touching, gesturing	role-play, drama, movement, building things, sports and physical games, tactile experiences, hands-on learning
Musical	via rhymes and melodies	singing, whistling, humming, tapping feet and hands, listening	sing-along time, trips to concerts, playing music at home and school, musical instruments
Interpersonal	by bouncing ideas off other people	leading, organizing, relating, manipulating, mediating, partying	friends, group games, social gatherings, community events, clubs, mentors, apprenticeships
Intrapersonal	in relation to their needs, feelings, and goals	setting goals, meditating, dreaming, planning, reflecting	secret places, time alone, self-paced projects, choices
Naturalist	through nature and natural forms	playing with pets, gardening, investigating nature, raising animals, caring for planet earth	access to nature, opportunities for interacting with animals, tools for investigating nature (e.g., magnifying glasses, binoculars)

The next model comes from Rita Dunn.[6]

Analytic Tendencies	Global Tendencies
Makes decisions based on sequential logic	Makes decisions based on feelings and intuition
Is detail oriented	Sees the *big picture*
Facts and data rule	Imagination rules
Words and tests impress	Symbols and images impress
Emphasizes present and past	Emphasizes present and future
Often excels in math, science, grammar, spelling, and computer technology	Often excels in the arts, philosophy, psychology, and religion
Believes in facts	Believes in emotions; "gets" ideas
Takes pride in knowing	Takes pride in supporting
Appreciates order and patterns	Appreciates spatial perceptions
Understands objects' data and uses	Perceives objects' possibilities
Reality based	Fantasy based
Forms strategies	Presents possibilities
Improves existing things	Creates new things
Practical in orientation	Impetuous, impulsive
Makes safe life choices	Takes risks

The final model I would like to present is the Kunjufu Learning Styles Model. Keeping in mind that learning styles are 80 percent biologically imposed, my model is comprised of the following:

Chapter 4: Learning Styles

1. Visual Learners
   a) Visual-print
   b) Visual-pictures
2. Oral/Auditory Learners
3. Tactile/Kinesthetic Learners

Visual. There are two types of visual learners: visual-print (left brain) and visual-pictures (right brain). Lesson plans that depend on ditto sheets and textbooks favor the visual-print learner. However, lesson plans that use textbooks and ditto sheets exclusively will not meet the needs of visual-pictures learner. This type of learner will understand the lesson better if it's presented in pictures.

Remember flashcards? Both types of visual learners can benefit from using flashcards, but it might help the visual-pictures learner if the "flash" were taken out of the card. Visual-pictures learners learn best when they can look at pictures for long periods of time. A picture really is worth 1,000 words.

Oral/Auditory. At first glance oral and auditory learning styles seem so similar as to be one and the same. They do work closely together; when you speak, you hear. Students who fall into this category, however, experience these modalities differently.

Oral learners love to hear the sound of their own voice. It's like music to their ears. These are the students who love to talk, and there's a reason for that. Speaking helps them to learn. It helps them think. Reading aloud helps their fluency, retention, and comprehension of information.

Auditory learners learn best when they can hear the lesson, but don't force them to read aloud unless you're confident that they won't be embarrassed. Give them a book, headphones, and a book on tape, and they're in their learning element.

You'll find that students in this category may have both modalities, but if you observe closely you will notice that one modality will probably dominate.

Tactile/Kinesthetic. Tactile and kinesthetic are often used interchangeably in the literature, but they are extremely different. As long as a tactile learner is working with his hands, he can learn while sitting still. Not true for the kinesthetic learner. A tactile learner learns best when he can touch or take an object apart, when he can doodle, when he can use his fingers to read and do math. For some reason, we don't have a problem with women sewing, knitting, or crocheting while listening to a speaker, but we forbid African American males from holding a ball in their hand or doodling while they are reading or listening to a lecture.

In contrast, a kinesthetic learner needs to be able to stand, pace, and move around. Have you ever seen a male who, while sitting down, just couldn't keep his legs still? That's a lot of pent up energy. He'd feel better if he got up and moved around. When forced to sit still for extended periods of time, kinesthetic learners get fidgety. Their energy builds to a point where they need to release it by moving around. Kinesthetic learners may also like to dramatize their points by gesticulating and using highly energetic body language.

As you observe the students in your class, keep my learning styles model in mind. Make a chart that will enable you to easily see how your students fit into the six categories. Feel free to adapt the following for use in your classroom.

Chapter 4: Learning Styles

Visual Learners	Oral/Auditory Learners	Tactile/Kinesthetic Learners
Visual-Print: 1. 2. 3. 4.	**Oral:** 1. 2. 3. 4.	**Tactile:** 1. 2. 3. 4.
Visual-Pictures 1. 2. 3. 4.	**Auditory** 1. 2. 3. 4.	**Kinesthetic:** 1. 2. 3. 4.

Keep this chart on your desk as a memory aid. As you get to know your students' learning styles better, you may need to make adjustments from time to time. Maybe Malcolm isn't a tactile learner as you thought at the beginning of the school year. He's really a kinesthetic learner. Make notes by their names. Now you're beginning to tailor your pedagogy to meet your students' learning needs. That's what Master Teachers and Coaches do. Believe me, as you grow in your knowledge of how your students learn, teaching will become a joy.

One way to better understand your students' learning styles is to assess your students. For example, let's say you want to know what your auditory learners respond best to: lectures, stories, or rap tunes/music videos. Simply decide on your topic, then deliver the lesson in the three formats: a 20-minute lecture, a 20 minute-story, and a 20-minute session of rap and music videos.

Next, have the students write about what they remembered about the lecture, the story, and rap CD. This exercise will give you a greater appreciation of the format that works best with your auditory learners: lectures, stories, or rap tunes/ music videos. Experiment with different formats that target the other learning styles.

Next, take out last week's lesson plan and review honestly and objectively. Ask yourself the following questions:

- How many students' needs did you meet with last week's lesson plan? That's easy to figure out. How did they do on their quizzes, tests, and in-class assignments?
- Did they turn in their homework? How did they do?
- How was their classroom behavior?

I would like you to consider taking your students off textbooks and ditto sheets once a week. If we are truly going to meet the needs of Black male students, the least we can do is wean ourselves from textbooks and ditto sheets once a week.

If at least two-thirds of your students are visual-pictures, oral, auditory, tactile, and kinesthetic learners, it should be obvious that you are now approaching the national proportion of 80 percent or more of Black male students who may not be visual-print learners. In contrast, teachers use ditto sheets and textbooks 90 percent of the time.[7] Is it any wonder that Black boys are struggling in school?

We could reduce special education placements and maximize Black boys' educational experience if we simply wrote 80 percent or more of our lesson plans for visual-picture, auditory, oral, tactile, and kinesthetic learners. How unfortunate that we have written 90 percent of our lesson plans for just one group: visual-print learners.

Chapter 4: Learning Styles

Learning Centers

Great schools often incorporate learning centers in their classrooms. I would like you to create six learning centers in your classroom with activities for the following:

- Visual-print learners
- Visual-pictures learners
- Auditory learners
- Oral learners
- Tactile learners
- Kinesthetic learners

This is where the rubber meets the road.

One of the most challenging aspects of my work is helping teachers set up classroom learning centers. There are two major reasons for this. First, there's a lot of work involved in creating learning centers. Second, the cost for materials may seem prohibitive. Given our economy, that can be a challenge for teachers.

I'm reminded of poor people who try to convince me that they can't afford to buy fruits and vegetables, that it's cheaper to buy baloney and candy and potato chips. I remind them that it's more expensive to treat high blood pressure, heart disease, cancer, and diabetes.

For some reason we have a problem spending $50 for each learning center, but we have no problem sending these boys to special education where the cost is $20,000 or more per child—and if that doesn't work, spending $30,000 to incarcerate them.[8] You do the math. $50 per learning center, $20,000 for special education, or $30,000 for prison. To me it's a no brainer. Learning centers are the most cost effective solution to meeting the learning needs of our boys.

Are our schools designed for children, or do the teachers, budget, and unions come first?

The second concern teachers have is that learning centers stimulate a lot of movement in the classroom. Yes, as students move from station to station there will be movement, energy, and fun. There will be talking and sharing of information. Students will ask questions. Some teachers want their students sitting still all day, and unfortunately some administrators give high marks on evaluations for maintaining a still, quiet classroom.

Imagine a classroom where some 30 students are moving from one learning center to the next. Outsiders looking in would probably be shocked to see what appears to be a chaotic room. But I think it's worse to have 30 zombies in a class that are bored, not asking questions, and not on task. I would much prefer a somewhat noisy classroom filled with students who are excited about learning than 30 zombies.

A large percentage of African American males are tactile and kinesthetic learners. Of all the learning styles, this group is given the least attention and the most punishment. If we don't do anything else, we need to design classrooms that are conducive for tactile and kinesthetic learners.[9]

I encourage you to read Rita Dunn's work. She has provided a wealth of exercises and materials that will help you do a better job of teaching your tactile and kinesthetic learners.

But if you don't do anything else, can you at least allow a kinesthetic learner to stand up and work behind his desk? Can you let him walk around the classroom or in the back of the room as he reads his book? Can you let a tactile learner hold an object while he is attempting to do his work? Can you let a tactile learner draw or doodle while he is reading or listening to a lecture? These adjustments don't require any money or additional lesson plans from the teacher.

African American males who are tactile and kinesthetic learners are perhaps the most neglected student group, but it doesn't have to be this way. We can learn a lesson from affluent White parents. They often send their right-brain learners to Montessori schools, at least during the primary grades. These schools are set up to meet the needs of tactile and kinesthetic learners. Administrators, I recommend taking your teachers on a field trip to a local Montessori school. Take notes on how teachers manage their classrooms and the variety of learning modalities they must balance throughout the day. Afterwards, have a debriefing session with your teachers and brainstorm how the Montessori approach can be applied to your classrooms.

Physical Education

It is unfortunate, if not criminal, that your kinesthetic learners are given P.E. only once or twice a week for 20 minutes. All children, especially your kinesthetic learners, need P.E. five days a week for at least 45 minutes a day.

Instructions

Unfortunately, our school system has been reduced to high stakes testing. America is a test taking country. Grades are predicated on how well you perform on quizzes and tests, and your matriculation from one grade to the next is based on how well you do on state exams.

Many students fail at the very outset because of the tests' instructions. Teachers are aware of this, but most states will not allow teachers to read or interpret the instructions for their students.

The instructions and tests are designed for visual-print learners. If you are a visual-print learner, reading the instructions should not be a problem. On the other hand, visual-pictures, auditory, oral, tactile, and kinesthetic learners often struggle with written instructions and tests.

Whenever possible, teachers should read the instructions aloud to help students who are not strong print readers. Have your oral learners read the instructions aloud. The sound of their own voice will help them understand what is required to take the test.

Helping your tactile learners understand the instructions will be equally challenging. It wouldn't be appropriate in this kind of test for students to take objects apart nor can you use sign language, but try letting them hold something in their non-writing hand—a small, soft ball or another pencil, for example.

Exasperated teachers often tell their kinesthetic learners, "Stop fidgeting!" There is so much pent up energy that even when sitting their legs are constantly moving. Student athletes are often (not always) kinesthetic learners, and it is always amazing to me how we expect their sometimes bigger bodies to be comfortable while cramped at small desks and chairs. Teachers, when your kinesthetic learners stretch their legs, they're trying to get some *relief.* Can you allow these students to stand up, stretch, or pace in an area that won't disturb the other students?

The point here is that even understanding instructions is influenced by the learning style of the student.

Single Tasks or Multitasking

If you're a left-brain learner, you feel comfortable handling one task at a time. If you're a right-brain learner, you can handle many tasks at a time. If you're an analytical student, you focus best when there's only one task. If you're a global student, you enjoy juggling multiple tasks at the same time.

Our left-brain oriented classrooms are designed to handle one task at a time. For African American males, this is a recipe for boredom. Our boys are usually right-brain global multitaskers who can do far more than one operation at a time. If we were to visit a Black boy at home, he'd be listening to music on his iPod, talking to a friend on his cell phone, responding to a text message, and playing a video game. Is it any wonder that our boys fall asleep in school? Since your right-brain learners can handle it, begin to assign them multiple tasks.

The work of Rita Dunn reinforces this theory.[10]

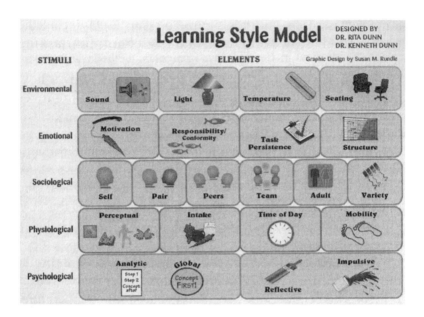

Dr. Dunn documented that learning style is tied to more than just the left or right hemispheres of the brain. It's even more than the components of my model. There's far more to meeting the needs of students than just simply adjusting lesson plans. We must begin to adopt a more comprehensive, macro approach to understanding and meeting the needs of students.

The Classroom Environment

Let us now look at how learning is affected by the following environmental factors:

- Sound
- Temperature
- Seating design
- Light and décor
- Time of day

Sound. Many teachers believe that an ideal classroom is a quiet classroom—no talking and no music playing in the background. However, right-brain, global, multitasking learners learn best when there is music playing in the background. There is excellent research that shows how playing classical or jazz music in the background improves academic achievement, especially for right-brain learners.[7] If more than 50 percent of your students are right-brain learners, you should begin to provide music in the background for your class. Or, allow students to bring their iPods to class along with headphones so that other students are not disturbed. One high school in Chicago plays classical music over the P.A. system as students walk the halls between classes. It has a very soothing effect.

Temperature. Research shows that female students prefer the temperature to be 76 degrees; boys prefer 69 degrees.[12] If there's no central policy regulating classroom temperature, then the thermostat will probably be above 69 degrees.

In older schools it's difficult, if not impossible, to regulate the thermostat. But if we want to maximize the learning potential of male students, we need to lower the temperature. Suggest to parents at the beginning of the year to have students bring an extra sweater to school just in case it gets too cold. Another solution might be to adjust the temperature based on the time of day. In colder climates, start the day at a slightly warmer temperature and then gradually decrease the temperature as the day goes on, especially after lunch.

One of the most contentious points many married couples have to resolve is deciding on the temperature in the home.

Some couples decide that his level will be 69 degrees, and her level will be 76 degrees. That's feasible at home, but what's the compromise in the classroom?

Seating Design. Our classrooms need to have a more fluid seating design. This will be a tremendous challenge if the seats and desks in your classroom have been bolted to the floor for the past 100 years.

Seating design affects mobility and comfort. As they get older, boys will require more space, so the seating design must provide enough room for them to spread their legs and feel more comfortable.

Classrooms with small desks and chairs and narrow aisles remind me of airplanes. It can get very uncomfortable sitting in the middle or window seat. That's why so many experienced travelers prefer the aisle where at least a little movement is possible. The really experienced travelers prefer the exit row. We need to design our classrooms like the aisle and exit row seats in airplanes.

In my books *Black Students, Middle-Class Teachers* and *100+ (*and *200+) Educational Strategies*, I talk about the issue of teacher-student proximity. Research shows that if teachers do not like certain students, they will not sit or stand close to them.[13]

Where do your students sit in your classroom, and where are you? Let me guess: the boys are sitting in the rear, and you are sitting in the front. Do you ever walk to the back of the classroom where most of your male students are sitting, or do you just focus on the front rows? We need to have a seating design that is family oriented and comfortable for all.

My favorite classroom seating design is where the students sit in a semi-circle around the room, and the teacher is in the center of the circle. In this design, the teacher is in close proximity to all the students. This design also allows the male students to stretch their legs.

Light and Décor. Right-brain, global, visual-pictures learners need rooms that are bright, encouraging, and full of color. One of the major reasons for the decline in African American students' scores after the fourth grade is that their classrooms are so drab, sterile, and dark that they literally destroy the zeal of the students. I don't know who told upper grade teachers that they should not decorate their classrooms, but if we want to maximize the potential for African American males, we need to create rooms that are stimulating and bright.

A White female teacher once told me that when it came to her students, she didn't see color. She saw children as children. I asked if I could visit her classroom. In her multiracial class, I saw an all-White Dick and Jane bulletin board, library collection, and poster set—but she said she didn't see color. I encourage you to purchase our poster sets so that children can see positive role models who look like themselves in your classroom.

This is also common in the high school classrooms of Instructors who only teach subjects, not students. They don't see why bright colors or motivational posters around the classroom are necessary.

Time of Day. When you find out the time of day when your students are most engaged with the lessons, then you will think twice about giving a state exam Monday morning at 8:00 a.m. Many upper grade and high school students do not get an adequate amount of sleep. According to several studies, high schools that delay the start time of tests show an improvement in school attendance and in some instances, in scores as well.[14] Master Teachers know that there are certain times of day when their students are more focused. They know when concentration levels are highest—before or after breakfast, and before or after lunch.

When we read at home, most of us are not sitting at a sterile desk for long periods of time without something to drink or snack on. If sitting in a comfortable environment, reading at a certain time of day with something to drink or snack on improves your concentration, why don't you do the same for your students?

Average Retention Rate After 24 Hours[15]

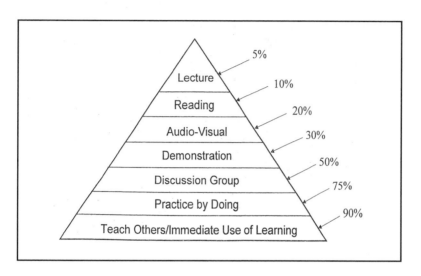

As the illustration indicates, students retain various kinds of instruction at varying rates according to how the instruction is presented to them. If we know that students will only retain five percent of what they heard from a lecture, why do we give so many lectures?

If we know that students will retain only 10 percent of what they read in a textbook or ditto sheet after 24 hours, then why are so many teachers using textbooks and ditto sheets?

On the other hand, 75 percent of all learners and even more tactile learners will retain more after 24 hours if they can actually perform the operation with their hands. Why, then, are we not providing more lesson plans that would benefit tactile and kinesthetic learners and, according to the chart, visual and oral learners as well?

Is it true that our classrooms have not changed much in the past 100 years?

Are we truly preparing students for the 21st century using outdated textbooks, ditto sheets, and boring lectures?

I encourage you to reconsider your pedagogy. Since the evidence shows that students retain more from tactile and kinesthetic learning activities, then let's give our students more tactile and kinesthetic learning activities!

In the next chapter we will look at how peer learning improves the academic performance of Black male students.

CHAPTER 5: PEER LEARNING

I am a strong advocate of cooperative learning. Research shows that the peer group is the number one influence on our children.[1] Within the school environment, peer pressure can be positive. With cooperative learning, children can learn from each other. It is a humbling experience for teachers to observe students who can sometimes do a better job of teaching their peers than they can.

Cooperative learning activities should be implemented in every classroom. African American males do everything together but study. All social, athletic, recreational, and entertainment activities are done either in pairs or groups. School is the only place where males work individually. With cooperative learning activities we can improve academic performance, and we can negate the idea that being smart is acting White.

Black boys are very competitive. Cooperative learning can be used in a competitive context to maximize academic achievement. For example, let's say that a classroom has 20 students. Divide the students into five teams of four. Each team should have a mix of ability levels. In other words, each team could have an A student, a B student, a C student, and a D student. In basketball, the team values a Kobe Bryant and a LeBron James. On academic teams, the A student is no longer viewed as a nerd. Teams are valuing the A and B students because they are the key to winning. By the way, prizes and incentives inspire academic achievement.

The buddy system is another way to leverage peer dynamics. In a classroom of 30 students, create 15 pairs. They then become responsible for each other. On one hand, boys are working in pairs with their buddies or in a larger group setting of four to five students. Now watch them soar as they compete against the girls. Boys do not like losing, and they definitely do not like losing to girls. Spelling bees, math contests, science fairs, history bowls, and any other academic activities that can be created as a game are perfect. I am reminded of the literature that states that if you let Black students think that quizzes and tests are really games, not only do they relax, their competitive juices rise, and they perform much better.[2]

We need to use the strengths of male culture, including the love of socializing and competition, to improve academic achievement. One of the major reasons for the success of KIPP schools is they use positive peer pressure to reinforce academic achievement.[3] The class with the best test scores, attendance, books read, and less disciplinary referrals receives substantial prizes.

Peer Teaching

In the American classroom, teachers tend to be the sole source of instruction. When students have difficulty learning the lessons, it is assumed that they were not paying attention. I wonder how much of that assumption is driven by ego.

Some students are simply incapable of learning from an adult, even from Master Teachers and Coaches. These students are uncomfortable learning from authority figures, and they are afraid to fail in front of their peers. As a result, they can become too tense to concentrate.

These students can benefit from learning with peers. Does it matter whether students learn from teachers or from each other, as long as they learn and do well academically?

Peer teaching also can help bring the student-teacher ratio to a more effective, acceptable level. In many inner city schools, the student-teacher ratio exceeds 28 to 1. Research shows that the ideal ratio is 17 to 1.[4] Few inner city schools possess that ratio.

Rap Music

After the peer group, the second greatest influence on children is rap music. (Interestingly, 70 percent of all rap music is purchased by White youth.)[5] If our children can memorize words from a rap CD, they can also remember the Constitution, the names of all 50 states, algebraic equations, and more. Children learn in different ways. The million-dollar question is: Can teachers put aside their ditto sheets, textbooks, and lectures and come up with new methods that incorporate the many different ways children learn?

Since African American males have such a strong interest in rap music, let's use this interest in our pedagogy and curriculum. Most African American youth seem to possess selective auditory skills. Lectures bore them, but they can repeat rap songs verbatim. Consider using rap CDs rated PG and PG-13 in your classroom, and let the lyrics serve as the source of that week's vocabulary words and social studies project. Set multiplication tables and anything else that children must memorize to rap music.

Peer learning means that teachers do not need to create the assignments themselves. Ask students how they'd like to incorporate rap into their assignments. They'll tell you they would like to develop their own Constitution rap, 50-states rap, and multiplication tables rap. Your students will love it.

I suggested this idea to some teachers. They said they gave their students an assignment and putting the concept to rap was optional. The students were resistant. The problem was that the teachers had not convinced themselves that this was a good way to teach the concept. If they had, they would not have made the assignment optional.

I asked, "Are homework assignments optional? Are taking tests optional? Then why would you make the rap approach optional?" Also, students may have resisted because the concept was boring and irrelevant, and they were not convinced it was important enough to learn. If teachers had explained the significance and relevance of the concept, the children might have been more eager to do the rap assignment.

Teachers often try to convince me that children have poor communication and verbal skills and that they are not auditory learners. When I point out that they are able to memorize a rap CD just by listening to it, most teachers will begin to see the light. Before saying that children have weak oral and auditory skills, teachers should look at the content of the information being disseminated. The students, particularly African American males, may not have poor communication skills. It could be that the subject of the lecture and the lecture approach are boring.

Peer Tutoring

In upper grades, peer tutors should definitely be used to help other students during study periods, lunch, and after school. They can tutor students in all subjects. They can even proof writing assignments and suggest areas for improvement.

In many cities, high school students are required to perform a certain number of volunteer hours during their high school years. Serving as a peer tutor not only helps strengthen subject knowledge, but the peer tutor can accumulate the desired number of volunteer hours needed to graduate through this service.

Students who may not feel comfortable asking questions of the teacher may feel perfectly comfortable admitting to a peer tutor that they don't understand a particular subject.

Schools teach more than reading, writing, and arithmetic. They teach values, and the value most emphasized is the individual over the community, "I" over "we." This goes against the grain of Black male culture. Most Black boys do not want to be recognized by themselves in the school assembly. They would prefer to stand on the stage with their buddy or cooperative learning group.

I strongly encourage you to read some of my earlier books on the Nguzo Saba and Maat. Given that these Africentric value systems embrace cooperation, they should be implemented by teachers of African American male students.

In the next chapter we will look at how gender influences academic performance.

CHAPTER 6: GENDER DIFFERENCES

Understanding how boys and girls learn differently may be the most important issue in this book. With such a disproportionate percentage of males placed in special education—almost a two-to-one ratio between White males and White females and almost a four-to-one ratio between African American males and African American females—it is obvious that we have not fully understood male learning styles and gender differences.

In my workshops for teachers I always ask if they know that boys and girls are different. Teachers will say yes, we know boys and girls are different.

If you know boys and girls are different, then…

1. How do you allow for those differences in the classroom? Do you teach to only one learning style or many?
2. Have you ever taken a course in male learning styles? Have you ever taken a course in *African American male* learning styles?
3. What are some of the differences between the ways boys and girls learn?
4. How do gender differences in behavior and cognitive ability affect learning?

Listed below are some general characteristics of boys that differentiate them from girls:

- More aggressive
- Higher energy level
- Shorter attention span
- Slower maturation rate
- Less cooperative

- Physically larger
- Influenced more by peer group
- Greater interest in math than reading
- Not as neat as girls
- Louder
- Distinctive walk
- Larger, more sensitive ego
- Hearing inferior to that of girls
- Gross motor skills more developed than fine motor skills

If boys are more aggressive than girls, how do we allow for that difference in the classroom?

If boys have a shorter attention span, what should we do differently when constructing our lesson plans?

Boys mature more slowly than girls. How do we respond to that difference in our classrooms?

If boys are more competitive, how does that change our pedagogy?

If boys are more influenced by their peer group, do we discipline them differently around their peers? How do we deal with the large, sensitive egos of boys?

If, on average, boys are not as neat as girls, should we allow for any differences in their notebook organizational skills?

If girls hear better than boys, how should we change our seating arrangements?

How do we allow for the fact that boys are more advanced in gross motor skills and girls are more advanced in fine motor skills?

In his book *Boy Writers: Reclaiming Their Voices*, Ralph J. Fletcher devotes an entire chapter to the issue of handwriting, fine and gross motor skills, and the differences between boys and girls.[1] Recalling his own boyhood, Fletcher says that when it came to handwriting, his teachers made no distinction between *what* he wrote and *how* he wrote it. Many years later, he conducted a survey of boys and asked them to answer the following question: "For me, the hardest part of writing is…." He thought the boys would talk about "the sheer drudgery of writing."[2] Instead they gave the following enlightening answers:

- My hand hurts.
- My hand gets sore (fourth grade boy).
- My fingers burn (third grade boy).
- Hand aches.[3]

A fifth grade teacher told Fletcher, "The first, most obvious thing I notice is that boys have a harder time writing neatly and quickly….Many boys comment that their hands hurt."[4]

It is not enough to theoretically know that boys and girls are different and not allow for those differences. If we are cognizant of gender differences, it is incumbent upon us to make the necessary adjustments (other than disproportionately placing males of all races and ethnic groups in special education).

Whether gender differences are genetic or caused by environmental factors (family upbringing, socioeconomic status, etc.) is being hotly debated and researched across many disciplines, including education. What do you think? Are gender learning differences due to nature or nurture? How much is genetic and how much is cultural?

Gender Learning Differences[5]
Brain Gender Differences

Part of Brain	Function and Differences	Similarities	Impact
Arcuate Fasciculus	Curving bundle of nerve fibers in the central nervous system	Likely develops earlier in girls as evidenced by their earlier speed capabilities	Females speak in sentences earlier than males
Broca's Area	Motor area for speech process; grammatical structure for word production	More highly active in females	Improved verbal communication skills in females
Cerebellum and Corpus Callosum	Contains neurons that connect to other parts of the brain and spinal cord; connects the two hemispheres of the brain	Larger in females	Females have superior language and fine motor skills; helps females coordinate the two sides of the brain better
Cerebral Cortex	Contains neurons that promote highly intellectual functions and memory; interprets impulses	Thicker in males on the right side of the brain; thicker in females on the left side	Males tend to be right brain dominant; females tend to be left brain dominant
Estrogen	Several female sex hormones that shape female brain	Much more present than males	In females, lowers aggression, competition
Testosterone	Male steroid sex hormone	Much more present and functional in males	Increases aggression and competition

An excellent article by Dr. Francis Wardle, "The Challenge of Boys in Our Early Childhood Programs," cites the following:

"Physical activity. In general, boys are more physical than girls. Far more boys engage in rough and tumble play than do girls. Boys also tend to enjoy physical activity on the playground, which is also cultural, as men in our culture engage in physical sports. Our boys' need for more physical activities is probably due to culture. It is neurological as well. The brains of boys develop slower than those of girls, even before birth. Further, on average, boys tend to be more aggressive than girls, a trend that appears in many cultures. Not only is this due to brain development, but also due to male sex hormones.

"Space. Boys simply take up more space than girls in their daily activities, both indoors and out. From the teacher's perspective they seem to spread out, use the far reaches of the playground, want to push the limits on field trips. Maybe this is one reason boys love to play and work on the floor.

"Kinesthetic learning. Learn through movement. Boys seem to thrive using kinesthetic learning, which fits well with the use of space needs for physical activity and their aggressive behavior. They love outdoor projects, gardens, building with units and hollow blocks, field trips and games.

"Hands-on learning. Boys are more advanced than girls in mathematical reasoning, spatial ability, and mechanical ability while girls score higher on memory, perceptual accuracy, verbal fluency, and language tasks.[6]

Janice Hale further explains why there may be a greater number of Black boys in special education, more than even White males. She offers the following:

"African American children are generally more kinesthetic than White children and have a higher level of motor activity. There is also medical evidence that African American males have a higher testosterone level than White males. African American children, particularly boys, should not be required to sit for long periods of time without an opportunity to spend energy."[7]

In my book *Countering the Conspiracy to Destroy Black Boys,* I use the following graphs to measure attention span.[8]

HYPERACTIVITY: A Diagnosis in Search of a Patient

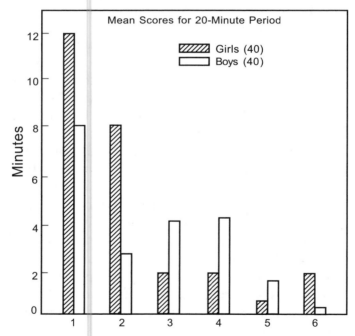

1-Longest Time Spent on One Activity
2-Time Spent in Teacher-Organized Activity
3-Time Spent in Construction-Toy Play
4-Time Spent Watching Others
5-Longest Time Watching Others
6-Time Spent Painting Alone

HYPERACTIVITY: Unraveling the Evidence

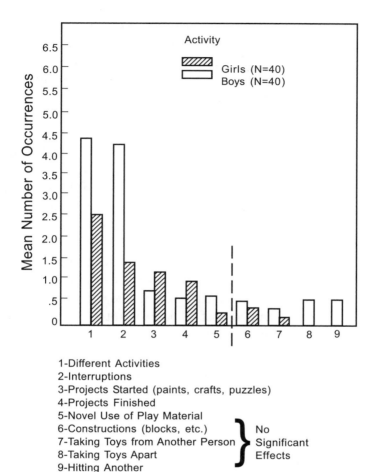

1-Different Activities
2-Interruptions
3-Projects Started (paints, crafts, puzzles)
4-Projects Finished
5-Novel Use of Play Material
6-Constructions (blocks, etc.) ⎫
7-Taking Toys from Another Person ⎬ No Significant Effects
8-Taking Toys Apart
9-Hitting Another ⎭

A psychologist and I were walking through a school and she commented, "Which boy is just being a boy and which one has ADD or ADHD, because I can't tell the difference." What a profound observation! They were just being boys.

"For many boys, the trouble starts as young as 5, when they bring to kindergarten a set of physical and mental abilities very different from girls'....Boys tend to have better hand-eye coordination, but their fine motor skills are less developed, making it a struggle for some to control a pencil or a paintbrush. Boys are more impulsive than girls; even if they can sit still, many prefer not to—at least not for long."[9]

I never will forget the kindergarten boy who, after his first week, told me in frustration, "You can't do anything in this class." He felt totally restricted in a classroom designed for females. He was looking for briefcases and empty boxes and hard hats and hammers and balls and trucks, but his teacher had not provided any of those things.

I wonder if this boy's frustration will lead to behavioral issues in the classroom that the teacher can't control. Will she refer him to special education? Will she retain him? Some school districts retain almost 20 percent of their kindergarten students, most of whom are male. While I am against social promotions, boys should not be retained because they mature academically at a slower rate than girls—yet kindergarten retention rates are increasing.[10]

"'Students that are behind are not equally behind in all things....So if one of the areas here is reading, then interventions like one-on-one tutoring in reading or early literacy does not mean that they need a whole grade reclassification. They need reading instruction reclassification.'"[11]

Attention Span
In an hour-long class, boys' attention span will average about 22 minutes. So what are the consequences of giving a 30- to 50-minute lesson to a student with a 22-minute attention

span? Should boys be placed in special education because the lecture is too long, or should the teacher shorten the lecture to create more alignment with the child's learning style?

The attention span of boys is short because of low serotonin levels.[12] So why are we forcing them to increase their attention span? Why not shorten the lecture and/or make the lesson more interesting and relevant? Reduce the use of ditto sheets and textbooks. When boys study subjects that interest them—sports, adventure, technology, automobiles, etc.—their attention span increases.

Maturation

What can we learn from the fact that boys mature more slowly than girls? From kindergarten through 12th grade, there is almost a three-year difference. Some schools are experimenting with putting eight-year-old boys in classes with six-year-old girls. In Germany, Switzerland, Belgium, and Hungary, the entrance of boys into elementary school is delayed until age six or seven. Unfortunately, in America parents use schools as a babysitting service, so I am not suggesting that we delay the entrance of boys into school because many parents would not know what to do with their sons. American schools can either allow for the maturation difference, place six-year-old boys in classrooms with five-year-old girls or provide single gender classrooms.

Maturation differences between boys and girls are expressed in many ways. Schools do not value how well boys can hold and manipulate big toys such as trucks and balls. They do value fine motor skills, such as the ability to manipulate pencils, pens, and crayons. Unfortunately, many schools expect five- and six-year-old boys to have the same level of penmanship as five- and six-year-old girls. Boys who are unable to write or color as well as girls are threatened with special education.

Since we know that on average girls hear three times better than boys, teachers should change their seating charts and put boys in the front of the class. The hearing issue, in addition to testosterone, helps explain why boys are so loud and why they respond better to a strong voice.

In the excellent book, *Equity in the Classroom*, edited by Patricia Murphy, the following insight is provided:

"Males tend to extract information from context while females tend to pay attention to context in a study of a problem.

- In considering male reasoning or other male problem solving, males tend to take analytical-rule-based approaches while females tend to take holistic approaches and emphasize empathy.
- Males tend to be more hasty, impulsive, and willing to take risks while females exercise more care and deliberation.
- Males tend to attribute success to their own efforts and failure to external factors while females do the reverse. The perception of personal failure may inhibit subsequent performance.
- Interactions among males, including their discourse, are marked by competition while females appear to prefer to work in cooperation. Their discourse is relational, the reference made to the previous speaker.
- Girls work in a concentrated way. Subject matter is worked through in half the time used by boys. Girls are well prepared.
- Girls keep strictly to the subject.
- Girls see the lesson as a shared venture.
- Girls listen and show respect when others speak.
- Girls are helpful to each other.
- Boys are active in an anarchistic way.

- Boys have a low degree of preparation.
- Boys broaden subjects and include new angles and points of view.
- Boys see the lesson as an individual matter.
- Boys constantly interrupt each other.
- Boys compete with each other in getting the teacher's attention."[13]

Before we continue, I am in no way suggesting that these differences are 100 percent universal. Not all boys are aggressive, have shorter attention spans, show slower maturation rates, exhibit more advanced gross motor skills, are less verbal, or can't hear as well as girls. But on average these are some of the gender differences. More importantly, it is obvious from the disproportionate percentage of boys in special education how teachers respond to these differences. Being different is not synonymous with being deficient. Boys and girls simply are different. Boys and girls each have unique strengths and unique challenges to deal with.

Other Differences
To serve boys in the classroom, teachers must be aware of and understand gender learning differences. Teachers must allow for those differences and make adjustments without resorting to putting boys in special education.

Boys have larger and more sensitive egos than girls. Boys with ADD or ADHD tend to be more oppositional and aggressive than girls and thus are more of a discipline problem with Instructors, Custodians, and Referral Agents. While 67 percent of boys with ADHD are diagnosed with Defiant Disorder (ODD), only 33 percent of girls are so labeled.[14]

Boys possess a greater propensity for rebelling against authority and engaging in conflict than girls, who are more likely to comply with authority and a hierarchical structure. The oppositional style of boys is seen as early as kindergarten;

in contrast, females tend to avoid conflict and seek to preserve harmony. In the book *Bad Boys*, Ann Ferguson makes the following observations:

"African American boys are not accorded the masculine dispensation of being naturally 'naughty.' Instead, the school reads their expression and display of masculine naughtiness as a sign of an inherent injudicious, insubordinate nature that is a threat to order that must be controlled. Consequently, school adults view any display of masculine mettle on the part of these boys, through body language or verbal rejoinders, as a sign of insubordination.

"In confrontation with adults, what is required from them is a performance of absolute passivity that goes against the grain of masculinity. Black boys are expected to internalize the ritual obeisance in such exchanges so that the performance of docility appears to come naturally. This is not a lesson that all children are required to learn, however. The disciplining of the body within school rules has specific race and gender overtones. For Black boys the enactment of docility is a preparation for adult racialized survival rituals of which the African American adults in the school are especially cognizant. For African American boys, bodily forms of expressiveness have repercussions in the world outside the chain linked fence of the school. The body must be taught to endure humiliation in preparation for future enactments of submission."[15]

When I was writing *Keeping Black Boys Out of Special Education*, I shared my ideas, concerns, and research with my colleagues. One of them very succinctly said, "The major problem in American schools is that we have not found positive ways to channel Black male energy."

That statement resonated with me because the percentage of Black boys in special education is simply too high and unacceptable. In fact, I almost wrote a full chapter just on Black male energy for this book. This is a major issue that needs to be resolved.

The Montessori teaching method uses a rich kinesthetic and experiential environment that helps children learn to learn. The emphasis is placed on manipulating materials, which certainly taps into the strength of the tactile learner. Unfortunately, Montessori schools are private and expensive and out of the price range of many African American students.

Fortunately, there has been an increase in the number of charter schools that use the Montessori method, and I encourage more founders to consider implementing the method in their schools. But because a large number of African American students will not attend a charter school, traditional schools should consider utilizing the Montessori method as well.

Physical Education

One of the important outcomes of Leave No Child Behind is that not only have art and music been virtually wiped out in schools, we have reduced, if not eliminated, P.E. These subjects are critical for right-brain learners, yet according to the Centers for Disease Control only 3.8 percent of elementary schools, 7.9 percent of middle schools, and 2.1 percent of high schools offer P.E. on a daily basis as of 2006.[16]

For kinesthetic learners, and in fact all children, it is crucial that we provide P.E. on a daily basis.

If you are concerned that offering P.E. will put reading and math scores in jeopardy, then you have not read the research. Eleven published studies analyzing data from approximately 58,000 students have found positive correlations between participation in physical activity and improved academic performance.[17]

A study conducted by the California Department of Education showed a significant relationship between academic achievement and the physical fitness of public school students. In another study where reading and math scores were matched with fitness scores of 353,000 fifth graders, 322,000 seventh graders, and 279,000 ninth graders, high achievement was associated with higher levels of fitness in each of the three grade levels. Studies done in Australia and Korea also found that P.E. improved academic achievement.[18]

According to various international ranking systems (e.g., Organization for Economic Cooperation and Development), America's academic performance has dropped significantly among industrialized nations.[19] In one list, the U.S. didn't even place among the top 25 countries in reading, math, or science.[20] I believe the reduction of P.E. classes in public schools is a major culprit. Exercise must once again become a regular part of school programs.

There are now schools being built without playgrounds. Can you imagine a school without a playground? Can you imagine the impact that has on all students, especially kinesthetic learners? How can we build schools without playgrounds in light of the research showing that as you increase P.E., you increase academic achievement?

Research shows that if time is taken away from reading instruction to allow for P.E., students still score higher in reading and math. As much as I am an advocate of time on task, here is evidence that says you cannot force students, especially kinesthetic learners, to stay focused only on reading and math for the six-hour school day to the exclusion of physical education.

Not only have P.E. programs been reduced, many schools have eliminated recess. The least we can do is provide periodic stretch breaks throughout the day. Research shows that when teachers provide recess or stretch breaks, students improve academically.

Investigators in Georgia studied the effects of an activity break on classroom behavior in a sample of 43 fourth grade students. Students exhibited significantly more on-task classroom behavior and significantly less fidgeting on days when an activity was scheduled than on non-activity days.[21]

A research project in North Carolina evaluated the effects of providing 243 students in kindergarten through fourth grade with a daily 10-minute activity break. Researchers found that the daily break increased on-task behavior by an average eight percent. Among the least on-task students, the activity breaks improved on-task behavior by 20 percent.[22]

In a New Jersey study with 177 elementary students, researchers compared concentration test scores after students completed either a classroom lesson or a 15-minute physical activity session. Fourth grade students exhibited significantly better concentration scores after completing the physical activity.[23] I commend the large numbers of affluent White families who demand the return of morning and afternoon recess and greater PE or they would remove their children from the school. I am still waiting for African American parents to demand the same.

Single Gender Classrooms

In 1985, at the NABSE (National Alliance of Black School Educators) conference in Portland, Oregon, I recommended implementing single gender classrooms in schools in my keynote address. I received tremendous opposition. It has only been in the last decade that our society has seen the need to provide single gender classrooms for boys. One major reason is because White feminists have found that if single gender classrooms are provided for females, their chances of pursuing careers in math and science are increased. For years, feminists have been frustrated by the fact that White females outperform White males K-12, yet White males still earn more money.

For the past 15 years I have been recommending that schools implement more right-brain classrooms. I now want to go on record with the following statement:

Less than eight percent of American schools provide P.E. on a daily basis. Clearly traditional schools are not equipped to meet the needs of kinesthetic learners. We need to provide schools exclusively for kinesthetic learners that offer P.E. on a daily basis.

The solution for kinesthetic learners is not Ritalin. The solution is providing movement, allowing activity, providing P.E. on a daily basis. Movement will help positively channel Black male energy.

Cooperative Learning

We discussed the value of cooperative learning at length in the last chapter, so here I'd just like to stress that boys and girls are different when it comes to learning either independently or cooperatively. Girls tend to learn independently, and boys tend to thrive when they are in a cooperative learning environment. Nature or nurture? I would say both. Now that's not to say that girls can't thrive in a cooperative learning group and that boys can't do well by themselves. But the research is clear on gender learning preferences.

As we've seen throughout this book, classrooms are oriented to the independent female learner, not the cooperative/competitive male learner. We would improve the academic performance of boys if we tapped into their cultural strengths and created more cooperative and competitive learning activities for them.

Homework

There's been a lot of discussion about the importance of homework. Some teachers believe that the more you give reflects the quality of the school. Others believe that homework should not be busywork.

Research shows that 84 percent of males either turn their homework in late or not at all. In contrast, only four percent of females turn their homework in late or not at all.[24]

Let me paint a clear picture. A male student receives an A on the mid-term and a B on the final exam but receives a D on his report card. How can that be? An A on the mid-term, a B on the final, and a D for the final grade. Not doing the homework was the culprit. On the other hand, doing the homework was not a precursor to doing well on the tests.

Do you feel disrespected when your male students do not turn in their homework? If they do well on in-class assignments, quizzes, and tests and the only problem is not turning in homework, should their report cards be used against them?

If boys are given homework that is not intellectually stimulating, they will take hours to complete it. They will view it as busywork, especially if they're earning A's and B's on exams. This kind of homework insults their intelligence. In contrast, if you give them a more challenging homework assignment, they will be more focused on completing it within a reasonable time frame.

If we really want to maximize the academic achievement of African American male students, we must become more cognizant of homework and its gender implications for male students. I strongly recommend that teachers consider implementing the following homework policies:

- Do not use low report card grades as a way to penalize boys for not turning in homework assignments. Let report card grades reflect the work students have done in class and at most, major assignments and special projects that have to be completed after hours.

- Let daily homework assignments serve as a way for students to earn extra credit points.
- Give less homework.
- Give more intellectually challenging homework.
- Give homework exercises that are based on lessons that were covered in class. Never give students homework that they don't understand, that they didn't learn about first in class. One reason why African American scores decline after fourth grade is because teachers expect parents to serve as their assistant teachers at home. This is a middle-class concept that does not take into account the fact that for many African American students, the at-home playing field is not always level. For example, to expect an illiterate parent to tutor a child in algebra, geometry, or trigonometry, biology, chemistry, or physics is unreasonable and extremely unfair.
- A peer learning approach would be to let students create homework assignments that interest them. Let your students know that this is how doctoral candidates in college earn their PhD's. They create their own program of research and study. Imagine your African American male students asking if they can write a music video or develop a business plan. Your job would be to help him develop the elements that would go into the assignment.

In the next chapter on mainstreaming strategies we will look at some of the ways Master Teachers have kept Black boys out of special education and in the regular classroom.

CHAPTER 7: MAINSTREAMING STRATEGIES

I will always be grateful to my late mentor, Dr. Barbara Sizemore, whose consulting paradigm—problem, causes, solutions, implementation—has enabled me to help school districts around the country develop effective educational strategies. I have used this model to help schools mainstream their Black male students. Reducing the number of Black boys in special education has been a major focus of my mission.

Listed below are strategies regular classroom teachers and administrators should consider before referring a child to special education.

1. Group children by gender.
*
2. Develop shorter lesson plans.
*
3. Assign shorter texts.
*
4. Allow more time to complete assignments and text.
*
5. Allow more physical movement.
*
6. Create learning centers.
*
7. Develop more right-brain lesson plans.
*
8. Implement cooperative learning opportunities in the classroom.
*
9. Keep lesson plans simple, brief, visual, novel.
*

10. Assign less homework.

*

11. Assign more meaningful homework.

*

12. Let children stand at their desks.

*

13. Allow children to hold objects.

*

14. Play music in the background.

*

15. Pair students together as learning buddies.

*

16. Identify a daily leader of the class.

*

17. Give oral exams.

*

18. Reduce the number of answers on multiple-choice exams.

*

19. Give open-book exams.

*

20. Read test instructions aloud.

*

21. Allow children to "set their stage" (greater prep time at their desks).

*

22. Arrange preferential seating.

*

23. Give frequent praise.

*

24. Review and assist students with notebook assignments.

*

25. Refer to students as Mr. and Miss.

*

26. Refer to students based on their career choices.

*

27. Start each day with, "This day in Black history."

*

28. Provide a daily word problem.

*

29. Have a positive section of the board with the students' names.

*

30. Compile positive attributes for each student.

*

31. Use rap CDs and videos in learning activities.

*

32. Connect math to the NBA, NFL, and rap sales.

*

33. Allow students to play chess and checkers.

*

34. Decorate the wall with student photos.

*

35. Reduce the student-teacher ratio.

*

36. Allow children to learn on the floor, sofa, and other relaxed positions.

*

37. Encourage children to ask "why?"

*

38. Make the curriculum more culturally relevant.

*

39. Allow an angry student 60 to 180 seconds to calm down.

*

40. Create an area in the classroom for a student to express his anger.

*

41. Encourage students to put concepts to rap.

*

42. Create a classroom that's full of bright colors and designs.

*

43. Make sure students exercise on a daily basis.

*

44. Provide periodic exercise throughout the day.

*

45. Provide a martial arts class.

*

46. Always use visual aids.

*

47. Provide recess and a playground.

*

48. Allow for penmanship variances.

*

49. Allow students to print if they cannot write in cursive.

*

50. Allow information to remain on the overhead projector or chalkboard indefinitely.

*

51. Provide more books on tape.

*

52. Assign books that are especially interesting to boys.

*

53. Stock classroom and school libraries with books that boys will find interesting.

*

54. Allow the use of calculators.

*

55. Give brief instructions.

*

56. Avoid nagging, lecturing, arguing, sarcasm, yelling, and slipping into power struggles.

*

57. Reward good behavior.

*

58. Discuss negative behavior in private.

*

59. Ignore minor issues.

*

60. Keep your voice calm.

*

61. Move from a teacher-centered pedagogy to a student-centered pedagogy.

*

62. Understand that children want attention.

*

63. Allow students to water plants, care for pets, and perform other classroom management activities.

*

64. Create the maximum amount of space between each student.

*

65. Determine the best day and time for taking tests.

*

66. Avoid timed tests.

*

67. Position your desk in the center of the room.

*

68. Sit with children.

*

69. Allow students a choice of assignments.

*

70. Provide assignments at different grade levels.

*

71. Refer to tests as games.

*

72. Create a relaxed section of the room filled with magazines, games, audiotapes, and videos to be used by students who have completed their work.

*

73. Enlist parent volunteers to work in class on a daily basis.

*

74. Ignore behaviors that do not disturb others.

*

75. Pick and choose your battles.

*

76. Create individual and classroom rewards.

*

77. Be flexible as students move from one activity to another.

*

78. Use good eye contact.

*

79. Use hand signals.

*

80. Present well-prepared and organized lesson plans.

*

81. Provide time for students to get organized.

*

82. Utilize outdoors for classroom experiences.

*

83. Keep extra pencils, paper, and books in a designated area.

*

84. Assign room captains to collect homework and coordinate assignments.

*

85. Provide equitable response opportunities.

*

86. Provide equal feedback.

*

87. Use Native American hand wrestling to resolve conflicts.

*

88. Invite male role models on a weekly or monthly basis to speak to students.

Africentric approaches should definitely be incorporated into classrooms, schools, and school districts where there is a majority of African American students. Indeed, all students will benefit from the African approach to learning.

1. Teach children the Nguzo Saba. When implemented in the classroom, these seven African values will reduce disciplinary problems and fighting and increase self-esteem. The Swahili words for the seven values are *umoja* (unity), *kujichagulia* (self-determination), *ujima* (collective work and responsibility), *ujamaa* (cooperative economics), *kuumba* (creativity), *nia* (purpose), and *imani* (faith). Put these seven principles on a poster and review on a regular basis. The Nguzo Saba and Kwanzaa should be celebrated not just in December but throughout the year.
2. Maat also should be taught throughout the year. The seven cardinal virtues of Maat are truth, justice, order, harmony, balance, reciprocity, and righteousness.
3. Unity-criticism-unity is a peer disciplinary session that uses peer pressure for positive ends. To begin, children form a circle. Each child makes a positive statement about another student. The session can also open with a chant. Next, the children who want to offer criticism raise their

hands and offer criticisms. The child being criticized cannot respond. We must teach children self-control. In addition, the person giving the criticism can only criticize the behavior, not the person. After all criticisms about a particular child have been heard, the child being criticized can respond. Upon completion, the students determine who was right and who was wrong. They decide, based on the range of punishments available to them, what punishment, if any, the child should receive. To close the session, children can offer praise to a particular child or each other, or they can sing and chant.

These strategies are effective ways to stem the tide of special education placements. Before another African American male child is placed into special education because of behavioral issues, reading difficulties, and other issues that do not warrant such a drastic measure, the regular classroom teacher should implement these activities under the supervision of an administrator. This would be included in the IEP. To avoid excessive special education placements, the wealth of information available on mainstreaming children into regular classrooms should be studied and implemented.

In the next chapter we'll discuss the crisis in reading scores among African American males and what we must do to close the racial academic achievement gap.

CHAPTER 8: READING

Reading is the most important subject in our schools. You can't solve a math word problem without reading skills. You can't do well in social studies or science without a strong foundation in reading.

Reading is probably the subject least understood by educators, and it causes the greatest controversy in terms of the approach to be used.

Unfortunately, illiteracy is also the leading precursor of special education and prison.[1]

- **Any child who is 5 months or more behind in reading at the end of first grade only has a 20% chance of reading on grade level by 12th grade.**
- 80 percent of students who are recommended for special education placement are below grade level in reading.
- Only 12 percent of Black fourth grade boys are proficient in reading.
- 74 million Americans read below the eighth grade level.
- 85 percent of juveniles coming before the courts are functionally illiterate.
- 70 percent of prison inmates are illiterate.[2]

It is unfortunate that governors are now determining prison growth based on fourth grade reading scores. How asinine! Wouldn't it be cheaper to allocate $500 for a literacy program than $38,000 for prison which has a recidivism rate of 85 percent?[3] Clearly $500 is more cost effective than $38,000.

What is the best age to teach children to read? There are two schools of thought on this very important decision. Most educators feel that children should start reading in preschool and definitely by kindergarten and first grade. Others, and I'm included, believe that we are rushing children, especially boys of all races, to read before they are ready.

Earlier we mentioned that girls mature faster than boys, and most educators will agree. The million-dollar question becomes: How do we allow for those maturation differences in the classroom?

If we know that girls mature faster than boys, then why are we expecting boys to read at the same level as girls? Eighty percent of the children, mostly boys, who are placed in special education, are not there because of ADD or ADHD. They're there because they simply did not read at the same level as girls.

David Elkind writes in *The Hurried Child*:

"In Russia, formal education and instruction do not begin until children are age seven, and yet Russian children seem far from intellectually handicapped. Early reading, then, is not essential for becoming an avid reader. Nor is it indicative of who will become successful professionals. Jean Piaget cautioned about teaching reading or other academic skills too early before concept development has taken place. He warned that formal detailed instruction given too soon can interfere with normal learning development."[4]

Ideally, single gender classrooms make the most sense for our boys. We cannot afford any more boys being placed in remedial reading and special education because educators did not allow for maturation differences and because the system forces boys to read before they are ready.

Some concede that single gender classrooms should be implemented in fourth through 12th grade. While I'm not against that, I believe that single gender classrooms and schools need to be implemented even earlier, kindergarten through third grade. The current approach simply is not working. We put boys and girls together in the same classrooms even though girls are ready to read, or are already reading, and boys are not. This is not fair to our boys. When boys are forced to read before they are biologically ready, their brain will shut down to protect them.

There's nothing wrong with boys. Reading readiness is an issue that transcends race. White girls mature faster than White boys. Asian girls mature faster than Asian boys. Hispanic girls mature faster than Hispanic boys. Native American girls mature faster than Native American boys.

I strongly recommend the following:

1. Teachers of co-ed classrooms should allow for maturation differences between boys and girls in their lesson plans.
2. Administrators should design single gender classrooms beginning in the primary grades.
3. Boys and girls can be brought together when boys are reading at the same level as girls.

Reading Materials

More than 90 percent of American elementary school teachers are female. This becomes apparent in the selection of reading materials. I encourage you to visit your local school and look at the library collection and the books in the classroom from the perspective of a Black boy. Honestly, would a Black boy be interested in the materials?

How many African American male staff were involved in choosing which books would be purchased for your school library?

Not only have we designed a female classroom for male students, we also have selected reading materials that are more appropriate for female students.

Boys prefer nonfiction over fiction, yet many of the books in our schools are fiction. Boys do not like reading romance novels. They do not like reading long chapter books. Most boys are not interested in reading about people's feelings. They are interested in things and how they work.

Be honest. Do you read everything or do you read the materials that interest you?

Have you ever asked Black boys what types of books they would enjoy reading? If you had, they would have told you that they want to read books where they see themselves in the story. They like comics and books about sports, hip hop, technology, and cars. Boys read for information. They like it short, and they want to be able to read something that they can apply to their real life situations.

Teachers try to convince me that boys lack comprehension skills. Yet a boy can read the manuals for his iPod, Blackberry, video game, and any other high tech gadget and within 30 minutes has put the object together. Many adults do not understand the directions given in these high tech manuals. Boys read for information.

My company, African American Images, has created a collection of books titled *Best Books for Boys*. We have observed and listened to boys. We have provided literature and observed their reactions, and as a result, we've learned a lot about what they enjoy reading. *Best Books for Boys* is a collection of intellectually stimulating, culturally relevant, motivational books that have received great reviews from our young readers. Visit AfricanAmericanImages.com to purchase a set for your specific grade.

The Phonics-Whole Language Debate

For the past century, there's been a tremendous debate on how to teach *all* children to read. The two popular schools of thought are phonics and whole language. I'm reminded of Rudolf Flesch's book, *Why Johnny Can't Read* and the sequel, *Why Johnny Still Can't Read*. His premise was that Johnny can't read because America moved away from phonics and into whole language. I'm a strong advocate for phonics because to master reading, you have to be able to have the skills to attack the word. In whole language, a word is presented on a ditto sheet, and the student must memorize the spelling of the word or how the word looks. Whole language also includes a sight approach to reading, where a picture is shown with the word below.

What I respect most about phonics is that by third grade, there is literally no word a student cannot pronounce. A whole language student would have difficulty pronouncing *Jawanza Kunjufu,* but if you understand phonics, then you can sound the words out.

America moved toward whole language because publishers make more money with whole language, word, and sight approaches to reading. Phonics is labor intensive. Teachers who are serious about their craft will allocate extra time to teaching phonics.

I enjoy being a researcher and writer because I have to look at data squarely and ask myself, How does this finding affect my position? When I wrote *An African Centered Response to Ruby Payne's Poverty Theory*, there was a lot of data before me showing a direct correlation between income and academic achievement. If you increase income in the home, you increase academic achievement. Despite that research, I still believed that I could identify schools and an even larger number of classrooms in low-income areas where students were testing well above the national average.

It's not that I don't respect income as a factor. I just believe that even if your students are from low-income homes, they can still learn. You can still be an effective educator.

I had to face this same dilemma when I wrote *Reducing the Black Male Dropout Rate.* The research says that if you retain a child once, there's a 50 percent chance that he will drop out. If you retain a child twice, there's a 90 percent chance the child is going to drop out.[5] Despite those findings, I'm not in favor of social promotion. I have major problems when a ninth grader is not able to read beyond a fifth or sixth grade level.

In fact, some studies have found that if you retain a child and help him reach grade level, there's a 70 to 80 percent chance that he will graduate.[6] Schools will make the extra effort only when they begin to understand that both the child and the school failed. It's asinine for a school to retain a child and give him the same teacher, same curriculum, same pedagogy and expect a different outcome.

I'm on record as saying that I'm an advocate of phonics. Yet how can I maintain that position when phonics is excellent for visual-print, auditory, and possibly oral learners, but not so for visual-pictures, tactile, and kinesthetic learners? Phonics is conducive for left-brain, analytical, sequential thinkers, but it is not the best method for right-brain, global learners who do not think sequentially.

The following chart shows which reading techniques work best for the various learning styles.

Reading Techniques	Learning Styles
Whole language	Visual-print
Reading aloud	Oral
Phonics	Visual-print
Sight	Visual-pictures
Word	Visual-print
Listening	Auditory
Tracing	Tactile
Floor games	Kinesthetic

Which reading techniques would be most effective with your African American male students, with your visual-pictures, auditory, oral, kinesthetic, and tactile learners? One size does not fit all. Your students will benefit from different reading methods, and that means being sensitive to the variety of learning styles in your classroom. For a period of time we believed phonics was the right approach. Then whole language replaced phonics. I believe that both should be included in the curriculum. When we put children first—not educators, publishers, or budgets—our choices become clear.

What is the best way to teach African American males to read? One deficiency I had to accept about phonics is that visual-pictures learners may not be able to easily differentiate the multiplicity of mental pictures that are created by letters and letter combinations (e.g., diphthongs, digraphs, etc.). For example, what picture do you see when you read the letters *ga, th, ph, st, er, ly, sh, or ty*? How do you visualize *gh* as in *tough, through, cough*?

Auditory learners may also be challenged by the phonics approach. Do you realize that there are nine different sounds just for the letter *o*? For example, pronounce the words *tot, vote, toot, book, ton, town, boy, poor,* and *lesson.*

Reading Aloud

Teachers like to have students read aloud. This reminds me of schools that believe that the best way to measure learning is with true-false and multiple choice exams. These types of tests are ideal if you want to produce employees to work in factories. It is the most efficient way to evaluate learning in classes of 24 or more students. But what professions other than broadcasting will require you to read aloud?

Let me give an example. Michael is typical of many right-brain and ADD children who find reading, particularly reading out loud, a tremendous source of frustration and embarrassment. When Michael sees a word, he translates it into a mental picture and then verbalizes it. Because he tends to get easily distracted and processes information more randomly, his eyes may jump ahead or behind the word he's trying to read. The result is choppy, nonfluent reading. He may miss the little words and skip lines. Once children like Michael understand how to turn words into mental pictures, they become exceptional silent readers.

What is the best way to teach Black boys to read? Reading aloud may not be the best way to teach reading to visual-pictures, tactile, and kinesthetic learners. Reading aloud works best for oral and auditory learners.

David was found reading aloud on the lawn in front of his home. When asked what he was doing he replied, "I can only remember what I read when I hear the words." Since he had no one to read to and because he had heard that flowers might grow better when spoken to, he had decided to read aloud to the flowers.

David was correct about how he retains information. Although his fluency is good, he does not retain information unless he can also hear the words. If he listens to a book on tape, he learns easily. When he reads a book, however, either he or someone else must read the text aloud. Both auditory and oral learning styles are connected in David's case.

One day when David was in eighth grade, his teacher instructed the class to read a passage in a book and then explain it in writing. David moved his lips and spoke the words aloud. The teacher asked him to read silently. He explained that he had difficulty understanding what he was reading unless he heard the words. He asked if he could sit in the hall to read the information out loud. The teacher said, "If you cannot understand this book without reading it aloud, you ought to get remedial assistance." Needless to say, David felt humiliated.

This goes on far too often in American classrooms. David is an auditory/oral learner. Reading aloud and listening are the most effective ways for him to read, retain, and comprehend information. Unfortunately, in this particular class, reading excellence was not the objective. The objective was to read like a visual print learner. This is disastrous for many students.

For tactile learners, I recommend that teachers use the Orton-Gillingham reading approach.[7] What I respect most about this approach is that it allows tracing of letters and words. It also uses objects. This is the best approach for tactile learners.

For kinesthetic learners, I recommend floor games where students can jump or move from one letter or word to another. Floor games appropriate for use in the classroom are available at teacher supply stores.

Obviously, floor games may not be the most appropriate way to teach reading to upper grade students. Older kinesthetic learners should be allowed to stand up while reading. Let them walk around the room or in a certain section where the other students won't be disturbed.

Teachers need to pick and choose their battles. If you find that your kinesthetic learner is on task but standing up, why make sitting in the seat the war? If you find that your kinesthetic learner is on task and reading well while walking around, then let him do that—unless we really do feel that the ideal student sits all day.

Teachers can stimulate a love for reading through their classroom learning centers. Auditory learners can listen to books on tape. Oral learners can read aloud. Kinesthetic learners can work on the floor mat, walk around the room, or stand up. The tactile learner can use the Orton-Gillingham approach and trace words and letters. The learning center for visual-pictures learners should be stocked full of picture books, brochures, posters, and notepads for doodling. Last but not least, visual-print learners can enjoy whole language and phonics activities presented in all of the learning centers.

Before moving to the next chapter I again want to stress the fact that we have not allowed for the maturation differences between boys and girls. We're making boys in kindergarten read when they are not ready. I once gave a workshop in Minnesota, and a White female staff person, a brilliant Master

Teacher, said that she homeschooled her sons until they were ready to read. One started reading in third grade, and one was not ready until fourth. She said, "I know my school district. I knew that if I enrolled my boys before they were ready to read, it would have been a disaster." So she homeschooled the boys until they were ready to read, and now they are honor roll students.

Unfortunately, most African American parents do not have the luxury of staying at home to homeschool their children. African American parents are handing their boys over to school districts that do not recognize that boys and girls mature at different ages. One solution is to implement single gender classrooms in the primary grades.

We need to provide literature that's appropriate for boys. It needs to be stimulating, motivational, and culturally relevant.

We need to change our mindset that one size fits all. It's not whole language vs. phonics. A comprehensive program designed to support many learning styles will include whole language, reading aloud, phonics, sight, word, listening, tracing, and floor games. The other challenge is that most schools are designed to teach *how* to read in primary grades and assume you have mastered that in upper grades where content is the focus. We need schools equipped to teach reading in the intermediate grades. Unfortunately, most schools rather than teaching reading to intermediate students they have sent them to special education. The mantra that primary grades teach **how** to read and upper grades teach **what** to read is outdated and does not address the large numbers of students exiting primary grades illiterate. If schools only have a 20 percent efficacy in reading from grades 2-12 we must acknowledge the problem is systemic and not genetic.

In the next chapter we will ask one of the most important questions in this book: Who wants to teach African American males?

CHAPTER 9: WHO WANTS TO TEACH AFRICAN AMERICAN MALES?

Have you ever heard of the term "combat pay"? Some school districts are now increasing teachers' salaries if they will agree to teach in so-called "combat zones," i.e., low-income communities or low achieving schools.

It is amazing how unions and school districts will accept this "solution," but they do not accept paying more money to recruit and hire African American male teachers. Ironically, many African American adults are beneficiaries of Jim Crow. I am one of them. I was a student in the 1950s and 1960s. Many of my teachers were not allowed, because of Jim Crow, to work in the private sector (Wall Street, corporate America). As a result, many of our best Black minds were confined to work in classrooms or at the pulpit.

Since 1954, there's been a 66 percent decline in African American teachers.[1] There has been both a quantitative and a qualitative decline. Not only were our best Black minds in the classroom during the Jim Crow years, but our teachers *wanted* to teach African American children. They understood the children. They understood the culture. They bonded with the students. They knew the families. They encouraged the students.

Historically Black Colleges and Universities (HBCU's) are excellent teaching institutions that graduate our most successful students. For example, data for 2007 show that although HBCU's only have 12 percent of African American students, they produce 30 percent of African American graduates.[2]

If you're a racist you may believe that it is easier to graduate from Howard than Harvard. Then explain this: 75 percent of African Americans who go on to White schools to earn their graduate degrees were undergraduates at a Black college.[3] If Black colleges are inferior, then how could they produce 75 percent of the African Americans who go on to earn their graduate degrees at White universities?

It's a wonderful experience for college students to have African American professors, to have lunch with them, brainstorm with them, and be mentored by them. Unfortunately, for the 88 percent of African American students who attend White universities, it's possible that they can go four years and never experience an African American professor.

The same situation exists for K-12 students. Our students can go K-3, K-6, and K-8, and never experience an African American male teacher. Unfortunately, there are schools in America where there's not one African American male in the building—and if he's there, I'll wager he's a janitor first, security guard second, P.E. teacher third, administrator fourth, and upper grade classroom teacher last. Rarely will African American males experience an African American male primary or intermediate teacher.

Many boys have told me that they had their first African American male teacher in ninth grade. Remember, many of our boys are dropping out in ninth grade.

It has been an honor to encourage more than 1,000 African American males to become classroom teachers, and especially to teach in fourth grade classrooms. I believe fourth grade is the most critical grade for Black boys.

Is the future of the African American race dependent on White female teachers? Who wants to teach African American males? Do White female teachers want to teach African American males, or is it simply a situation where they did not secure a plum position in an affluent suburb? Are they simply buying time, working in the inner city while they await a suburban position?

Please do not misquote me, and please do not misunderstand me. I spend around three days per week throughout the year working with White female teachers who are sincerely trying to do their very best to improve the educational outcomes of African American children. It's not their fault that they are not prepared. They were raised in White environments. They took few, if any, classes on Black culture, Black learning styles, Black history in college. They did not student teach in the inner city, but now they are teaching there. They have received one to three days of in-service training. They were not given a mentor, and now they have some of the most challenging African American male students in the country.

That's not fair. That's why I spend three days a week trying to address this issue.

I am concerned about the disproportionate percentage of White female teachers. There could be some correlation to the fact that White girls are placed in special education the least and African American males the most.

Eighty-three percent of America's elementary school teachers are White and female; only one percent is African American male. Could the dearth of African American male teachers and the preponderance of White female teachers be a driving force behind large numbers of Black boys who are placed in special education?

Call Me MISTER

More than a decade ago, the Call Me MISTER program was founded in South Carolina, one of the poorest states in America. The MISTER program is headquartered at Clemson University in Clemson, South Carolina and is a response to the question that I'm raising in this chapter: who wants to teach African American boys? And why are there so few African American male elementary teachers?

Call Me MISTER (an acronym that stands for Mentors Instructing Students Toward Effective Role Models) works with more than 500 African American males in South Carolina, Florida, Kentucky, Missouri, Pennsylvania, and Virginia.[4] Young men who desire to become teachers receive scholarships through the program. If we are serious about addressing this issue, we need to provide scholarships to African American males who want to become teachers.

If we can do it in one of the poorest states in the country, surely we can do it in more affluent states, especially where the need is just as acute.

Call Me MISTER also provides mentoring. They bring in consultants like me to help students understand how to effectively educate African American male students.

I strongly recommend that every superintendent reach out to Call Me MISTER. Those same schools that love telling me they can't find African American male teachers should contact Call Me MISTER. All leaders should contact their local politicians to see if they can create a Call Me MISTER program in their state. This is only if we're serious about increasing the percentage of African American male teachers.

A better approach than providing combat pay is to have teachers in the classroom who want to be there! School districts should use their financial resources to recruit African American male teachers who want to teach our boys.

I was pleased when U.S. Secretary of Education Arne Duncan declared that we need to increase the number of African American male teachers.[5] It would be almost suicidal for me to make that statement in my workshops because I would appear racist. Hopefully, when a White male, who just happens to be the Secretary of Education, makes the statement, we will not look at the issue through the prism of race and gender but through our knowledge of how to educate African American male students. If it takes an Arne Duncan to be heard rather than me, so be it.

I want to share research from a White professor, Thomas Dee at Swarthmore College. His article is entitled, "Teacher's Race and Student Achievement in Randomized Experiment."

"In brief the result of the test score evaluations indicate that exposure to an own race teacher did generate some substance of gain in student achievement for both Black and White students. More specifically these results suggest that a year with an own race teacher increased math and reading scores by 3-4 percentile points. Notably the estimated achievement gains associated with an own race teacher exist for nearly all groups of students defined by race, gender and several observed student, teacher and community characteristics. Overall, the results of this study provide evidence that ongoing efforts to recruit minority teachers are likely to be successful in generating improved outcomes for minority students.

"The prior literature offers at least two general explanations why the racial pairing of students and teacher might exert an important influence on student achievement. These explanations are not mutually exclusive. One class of explanations involves what could be called passive teacher effect. These effects are triggered by the racial presence and not by explicit teacher behaviors. For example: one frequently cited reason for the relevance of a teacher's race is that by its mere presence the teacher's racial identity generates a sort of role model effect that engages student effort, confidence and enthusiasm. For example: it is possible for an underprivileged Black student in the presence of a Black teacher who encourages them to reach their full potential. Similarly, students may feel more comfortable and focused in the presence of an own race regardless of the teacher's behavior. An alternative class of explanation for the educational benefits of own race teachers, points to active teacher effects. Race specific patterns of behavior among teachers including allocating class time and interacting with students and designing class materials, may indicate that teachers are more oriented toward students that share racial or ethnic background. For example:

prior studies have indicated that Black students with White teachers receive less attention, are praised less, and scolded more than White counterparts.[6]"

Ruby Payne, the challenge to Thomas Dee's research on the significance of the racial background of the teacher, not family income, is that only 6 percent of America's teaching core is African American. According to Kozol, Orfield, and Holzman, since 1954 and integration, there has been a 66 percent decline in African American teachers.[7] I strongly recommend every state implement South Carolina's Call Me MISTER program. On most state campuses, they provide scholarships and mentoring to increase the paltry one percent of African American male teachers. I have been actively involved in their mentoring.

Dr. Dee's research clearly shows the quantitative perspective, the improvement in test scores based on the race and gender of the teacher. I enjoy looking at the research and then determining what my position will be.

I'm in full support of Dr. Dee's research. I'm in full support of African American male teachers working with African American male students. When I speak to school districts where the students are 80 to 90 percent African American and the staff is 90 percent White female, I'm frustrated when the teachers, arms folded, sitting in the rear, seem to say, "Make me listen to you." I spoke at a conference where the union rep wore a t-shirt that read, "Teachers first." After she spoke, I got up and said, "*Children* first." Speaking to White female teachers with tenure is even more challenging.

That's why this chapter is so significant to me. Who wants to teach African American male students? One of the major reasons for the success of Urban Prep (a single gender school in one of the poorest neighborhoods in Chicago that has a 100 percent graduation rate) is they have a 60 percent male staff.

Chapter 9: Who Wants to Teach African American Males

It's not about the race or gender of the teacher. It's about their expectations, time on task, subject knowledge and delivery, and classroom management skills. I have seen some incompetent African American male teachers who have low expectations, poor classroom management skills, and poor time on task and are ineffective with African American male students. And I don't see any time soon when schools will increase the number of *qualified* African American male teachers.

Is the future of the Black race in the hands of White female teachers? If so, then we need to do everything we possibly can to help them do a better job of teaching African American male students.

I was once brought into a school to fix the "bad" Black children. I asked the principal, who believed in the cultural deficit model, "Before we fix the bad Black children do you mind if we observe three classrooms—same students but three different teachers?"

The students were undisciplined and unruly in the first two classrooms. A White male teacher taught the first period, and a Black female teacher taught the second. The third period was taught by an elderly White woman who had been teaching for more than 30 years. In her classroom the children were focused and on task. They enjoyed learning, and there were no disciplinary problems. When I showed the videotape of the first two periods to the staff, they were nodding in full agreement. But you could have heard a pin drop when I showed the third period class. Then I simply asked, "Do you want me to fix the bad Black children, or should we look at teacher quality in this school?"

It was as if the students had learned to selectively maintain discipline. How did they know which teachers deserved their respect and which ones didn't?

With all due respect to Dr. Dee and Call Me MISTER, as much as I would like to increase the number of African American male teachers, I have to play the hand I'm dealt. The goal is to improve teacher quality across the board, and we have to work with those teachers who are currently on the front lines, working with our children. As of now, that means White female teachers. Since 83 percent of teachers are White and female, we need to do everything possible to empower that population to do a better job, and hold them accountable.

In the next chapter we will look at additional solutions that we have not provided thus far in this book.

CHAPTER 10: ADDITIONAL SOLUTIONS

1. Right-Brain Classrooms
2. Technology Center
3. Chess
4. Peer Teaching
5. Booker T. Washington/W.E.B. DuBois Role Model Program
6. Hip Hop Center

In this chapter I will discuss a few more strategies that teachers can utilize to fully engage Black male students in the learning process.

Right-Brain Classrooms

We've attempted to document that large numbers of African American male children are right-brain learners. If we cannot provide more learning activities for visual-pictures, oral, auditory, tactile, and kinesthetic learners in regular classrooms, the only other recourse is to design right-brain classrooms.

I'm appealing to all administrators to offer at least one right-brain classroom per grade. In this classroom, there would be no ditto sheets or textbooks. There would be no timed tests. I am sensitive to the fact that state exams are timed, and we can teach test taking skills to address this issue. But is it necessary to time all tests during the 36-week school year? It is not necessary, nor is it beneficial.

A right-brain classroom provides lesson plans that are conducive to oral, auditory, visual-pictures, tactile, and kinesthetic learners. This is extremely important in the area of math. Unfortunately, most math teachers teach to left-brain learners. They teach in the abstract. A right-brain approach would be to teach math in the concrete. In other words, show how concepts and formulas apply to the real world. Your Black male students may not be doing well in your left-brain math class, yet they can, without pencil, paper, or calculator, convert kilos to grams and grams to dollar bills. It's obvious these boys understand math. They understand NBA math, NFL math, rap math, and drug math. We need to teach math from a tactile perspective where the objects, preferably dollars and coins, are used to teach.

I strongly recommend that you read about the great work Robert Moses is doing in the Algebra Project. Also read our book, *How to Teach Math to Black Students*.[1] The Algebra Project and our book reinforce the importance of teaching math from a right-brain, tactile perspective.

I'm not confident that teachers in a co-ed classroom are going to provide an adequate percentage of lesson plans for right-brain learners. This is one attempt, besides single gender classrooms, to encourage teachers to push the envelope and use more right-brain lesson plans.

Technology Center

The technology center I'm proposing is more than just a computer lab. Yes, computers will be there, but the center will also have iPhones, iPads, access to YouTube, Internet access, Kindle, the ability to text, download, create PowerPoint presentations, and play video games. Right-brain learners are global learners and multitaskers. At home African American males will be listening to music on their iPods, talking on their Blackberry, playing video games, and watching *106 & Park* on BET, all at the same time. Believe me, they know exactly what's going on with each of their gadgets.

If we want to maximize Black male learning styles, we need to move into the 21st century and become more high tech in our schools. Too many of our classrooms have not kept up with technology.

Technology should be in all schools, not just affluent schools. I'm aware that some schools in the inner city were built 100 years ago, and few if any classrooms have been wired to meet the 21st century. Yet we must address this problem so that our schools can begin to provide the technologies our boys love to use.

One of the great educational tools that are available to us is YouTube. Imagine oral, auditory, and visual-pictures learners viewing a video lesson on YouTube and writing a report about what they saw.

Teachers, use PowerPoint presentations to stimulate your students' interests and quick thinking skills. The words on your slides should be large enough to see from the back of the room. By the way, don't pack a lot of words on the slides. This is a common mistake. Use brief, simple sentences, word lists, or even fragments. The slides should support your lectures, not the other way around. Most importantly, fill your slides with lots of bright, colorful, meaningful pictures. Intersperse your presentations with motivational quotes from famous African American scholars, scientists, activists, doctors, writers, artists, musicians, and educators. Familiarize yourself with the animation features on PowerPoint. You'll enjoy putting the presentations together as much as your students will love the novelty of you using this technology in the classroom.

If we want to reduce the dropout rate and make schools more exciting and culturally relevant, then we need to install technology centers in our schools.

Chess

Chess is ideal for tactile learners. In addition, there is excellent research showing that it improves the attention span and concentration skills. The American Chess Foundation documented a 17.3 percent increase in the test scores of students who were involved in chess classes.[2] Make sure to stock the tactile learning centers in your classroom with this wonderful, strategic, mentally challenging game.

Peer Teaching

Earlier we talked about having students work in pairs and cooperative learning groups. Let's push the envelope even further. I strongly recommend implementing peer teaching once a week, if not once per day. Jonathan, a high school senior at a small African American charter school, was asked by his teacher to teach a couple of classes on *The Matrix* and *Matrix Reloaded*. Jonathan was allowed to design his own lesson plans and quizzes. His self-esteem soared, and knowledge of the subject matter was strengthened. The students enjoyed learning from a classmate about a popular topic.

Booker T. Washington/W.E.B. DuBois Role Model Program

Booker T. Washington was the founder of Tuskegee University. He was a brilliant educator who believed in acquiring blue collar skills. In contrast, W.E.B. DuBois, a brilliant Harvard scholar, believed in acquiring white collar skills. There's been a big debate in the Black community around these two schools of thought, blue collar and white collar. It reminds me of the debate between phonics and whole language.

One size does not fit all. We need to draw from the strengths of both Washington and DuBois. I recommend that every school develop a Booker T. Washington/W.E.B. DuBois Role Model Program. One week invite a blue collar role model to speak to the students. The next week, a white collar role model can speak.

Schools tend to value white collar over blue collar. I don't know if you're aware of this but plumbers, carpenters, electricians, and bus drivers are paid very well. In contrast, you can have a B.A., M.A., and Ph.D. and be unemployed. I'm concerned about many schools not respecting blue collar trades. This role model program is an attempt to correct this bias and give boys options. This is extremely important for tactile and kinesthetic learners who may not have a desire to become a lawyer but who enjoy working with their hands and moving around. One of the major reasons for the success of HBCU's is their weekly or monthly speaker convocations. Schools should require each teacher to identify a role model to speak to the students.

Hip Hop Center

There has been a disconnect between African American culture and school culture. The Hip Hop Center is one attempt to bridge the two.

Teachers, you must take advantage of your students' interest in hip hop. One of the best ways to teach language arts is to have children watch the videos shown on *106 & Park* and then have them discuss and write about the subject matter. This assignment will connect school culture and language arts to students' hip hop culture.

I'm not asking you to become a rapper. Simply draw on the resources of your students. Whatever concept you are trying to teach, ask your students, especially those who are well versed in hip hop and rap, to help create the learning activity. Once the activity has been fleshed out, then you can design the rubric so that all students will know what is expected of them.

Publishers are beginning to realize that rappers have captured the minds, hearts, and ears of all students. Scholastic and others have created hip hop materials for use in the classroom. I strongly recommend purchasing our *Hip Hop Street Curriculum* from AfricanAmericanImages.com. This full curriculum uses hip hop to teach language arts, social studies, and critical thinking skills.

Many of your Black male students are brilliant rappers. Let them create raps about science, math, history, geography, and language arts.

EPILOGUE: THE IDEAL
BLACK MALE CLASSROOM

- Master teacher, preferably Black male, with high expectations, excellent classroom management skills, and understands the importance of time on task
- A single gender classroom
- A right-brain classroom
- 17 students or less
- 6 learning centers: visual-print, visual-pictures, auditory, oral, kinesthetic, tactile
- Technology center
- Famous pictures of Black males on the wall
- Portable desks
- Teacher's desk in the center of student semi-circle
- Cooperative learning groups and learning buddies
- *Best Books for Boys* in classroom and school library
- Photos of male students on the wall
- P.E. daily
- Water, juice, and fruit available for snacking
- Maximum 22-minute lectures
- 69 degrees
- Classical or jazz music in the background
- Academic competitions
- Question are encouraged
- Only open-ended questions are asked by teachers
- Two extra hours of academics and recreation
- Booker T. Washington/W.E.B. DuBois Role Model Program
- Chess and checkers
- Discipline model: unity-criticism-unity (from my book, *Developing Positive Self-Images and Discipline in Black Children*)[1]

- A maximum of 22 minutes of homework
- Homework is only one-tenth of the classroom grade
- Use money to teach various concepts
- Tests are given during the best day and time for students
- Only 20 percent of lesson plans use textbooks and ditto sheets

In the Introduction, I discussed the late Rita Dunn and the tremendous work she did to help us understand students' learning styles. When you're feeling discouraged about the performance of some of your Black male students and your ability to teach them, remember the rays of hope Dr. Dunn found in North Carolina and Louisiana. When school districts implemented a pedagogy that was congruent with children's learning styles, test scores dramatically improved: **in North Carolina, scores rose from the 30th percentile to the 83rd percentile. In Louisiana, scores rose from the 30th percentile to the 78th percentile.**[2]

When teachers begin to respect the innate intelligence of their Black male students and the many ways they learn, there will be improvement, not only in their test scores, but classroom behavior as well. We can, absolutely, close the racial academic achievement gap. This book has been an attempt to illustrate if we design our pedagogy congruent with students' learning styles we can improve academic achievement. The above is not the only way to improve educational outcomes. Research also documents we can achieve the above by raising educators' expectations, improving teacher quality, having greater time on task, more involved parents, reducing economic and racial segregation, and using a culturally relevant curriculum and single gender classrooms and schools.

END NOTES

Introduction

1. Kunjufu, Jawanza. *Keeping Black Boys Out of Special Education* (Chicago: African American Images, 2005). See also: Hibel, Jacob, et al. "Who Is Placed into Special Education?" *Sociology of Education,* October 26, 2010. http://www.soe.sagepub.com/content/83/4/312.full.
2. Rowland, Andrew S. and Dale P. Sandler. "Prevalence of Medication Treatment for Attention Deficit-Hyperactivity Disorder Among Elementary School Children in Johnston County, North Carolina," *American Journal of Public Health,* February 2002, pp. 231-234.
3. Jacob, Brian A. "Where the Boys Aren't: Non-Cognitive Skills, Returns to School and the Gender Gap in Higher Education," *Economics of Education Review,* vol. 21, 2002, pp. 589-598. See also "Indicator 27 (2010), Characteristics of Full-Time School Teachers," www.nces.ed.gov/programs/coe/2010/section4/indicator27.asp.
4. Golon, Alexandra S. "Teamwork: Working with Teachers and School Administrators to Meet the Needs of Gifted Visual-Spatial Learners," www.visual-learners.com/support-files/workwatchr.pdf.
5. Dunn, Rita. *What If* (Lanham: Rowman, 2007), p. 23.
6. *ibid.,* p. 102.
7. Payne, Ruby K. *A Framework for Understanding Poverty* (Highlands: aha! Process, Inc., 1996).

Chapter 1: The Problem

1. Steinhauer, Jennifer. "Maybe Preschool Is the Problem," *New York Times,* May 22, 2005. www.nytimes.com/2005/05/22/wwekinreview/22stein.html.
2. "Proficiency of Black Students Is Found to Be Far Lower Than Expected," *New York Times,* September 11, 2010. www.nytimes.com/2010/11/09/education/09gap.html?src=twt&twt=nytimesnational.

3. "Assessing the College Readiness in Reading of Eighth- and Ninth Graders," www.act.org/research/policymakers/pdf/EXPLOREreading.pdf.
4. Orenstein, Peggy. *Schoolgirls: Young Women, Self-Esteem, and the Confidence Gap* (New York: Anchor, 1994).
5. Kunjufu, Jawanza. "Black Boys and Special Education—Change Is Needed!" www.teachersofcolor.com/2009/04/black-boys-and-special-education-change-is-needed.html. See also: "Overrepresentation of African American Males in Special Education," www.jsc.montana.edu/articles/v4n16.pdf.
6. "Putting Kids Out of School," www.acy.org/upimages/OSI_Suspensions.pdf.
7. Greene, Jay P., and M. A.Winters. *Public School Graduation Rates. Civic Report 48.* (New York: Manhattan Institute for Policy Research, 2003). http://www.manhattan-institute.org/html/er_48.htm.
8. "Chicago Public Schools Flunk Black Students," *Chicago Reporter,* August 13, 2007. www.chicagoreporter.com/.../Chicago_Public_Schools_Flunk_Black_Students/. See also Elkind, David. *The Hurried Child* (Cambridge: DaCapo Press, 2001), p. 68.
9. "Proficiency of Black Students Is Found to Be Far Lower Than Expected," *New York Times,* September 11, 2010.
10. Dobbs, Michael. "Youngest Students Most Likely to Be Expelled," *The Washington Post,* May 17, 2005. http://www.washingtonpost.com/wp-dyncontent/article/2005/05/16/AR2005051601201.html.

Chapter 2: Framework

1. Freed, Jeffrey and Laurie Parsons. *Right-Brained Children in a Left-Brained World: Unlocking the Potential of Your ADD Child* (New York: Fireside, 1997). See also: "Reading and A.D.D. or ADHD," www.readinginstruction.com/readandaddor.html.
2. "Right Brain vs. Left Brain Learning Styles," *The SPD Companion,* December 8, 2006. http://www.sensory-processing-disorder.com/The_SPD_Companion-right-and-left-brain-learning-styles.html.

3. Kunjufu, Jawanza. "Black Boys and Special Education—Change Is Needed!" See also: "Overrepresentation of African American Males in Special Education," www.jsc.montana.edu/articles/v4n16.pdf.

4. De Carvalho, Maria Eulina. "The Role of the Family in the Production of School Outcomes: The Cultural Deficit Model," in *Rethinking Family-School Relations* (London: Psychology Press, 2000), p. 63. See also: Valencia, Richard R., ed. *The Evolution of Deficit Thinking: Educational Thought and Practice* (Abingdon: Routledge, 1997).

5. Rapp, David. "The End of Textbooks? What's Stopping Districts from Ditching Paper Textbooks for Good?" Scholastic.com, November/December 2008. http://www2.scholastic.com/browse/article.jsp?id=3750551.

6. "E-Learning 2010: Assessing the Agenda for Change," *Education Week,* April 28, 2010. http://www.edweek.org/educationweek_e-learning_2010_specialreport.pdf.

7. Freed, Jeffrey and Laurie Parsons. *Right-Brained Children in a Left-Brained World: Unlocking the Potential of Your ADD Child.*

8. Dunn, Rita. *What If,* p. 23.

9. Miles, Sarah B. and Deborah Stipek. "Contemporaneous and Longitudinal Associations between Social Behavior and Literacy Achievement," *Child Development,* February 6, 2006, pp. 103-117.

10. Gurian, Michael and Kathy Stevens. "Closing Achievement Gaps: With Boys and Girls in Mind," *Educational Leadership,* November 2004, pp. 21-26. http://www.ascd.org/educational-leadership/nov04/vol62/num03/With_Boys_and_Girls_in_Mind.aspx.

11. Flatow, Ira, et al. "Does Multitasking Lead to a More Productive Brain?" National Public Radio, June 11, 2010. www.npr.org/templates/story/story.php?storyID.

12. Goldhaber, Dan, Betheny Gross, and Daniel Player. *Teacher Career Paths, Teacher Quality, and Persistence in the Classroom: Are Schools Keeping Their Best?* National Center for Analysis of Longitudinal Data in Educational Research, August 2009. http://www.urban.org/UploadedPDF/1001432-teacher-career-paths.pdf.

13. *ibid.*

14. Schaefer, Ward. "Teachers Fire Back at Film [*Waiting for Superman*]," *Jackson Free Press,* November 10, 2010. http://www.jacksonfreepress.com/index.php/site comments/kryptonite_in_the_classroom_111010.

Chapter 3: Black Male Culture

1. "Richard Pryor: Biography," http://www.richard-pryor.com.
2. Kunjufu, Jawanza. *Countering the Conspiracy to Destroy Black Boys* (Chicago: African American Images, 1985).

Chapter 4: Learning Styles

1. Golon, Alexandra. *Visual Spatial Learners* (Waco: Profrock, 2008), pp. 87-88.
2. Kunjufu, Jawanza. *Keeping Black Boys Out of Special Education,* pp. 68-69.
3. See: Kunjufu, Jawanza. *Black Students, Middle-Class Teachers* (Chicago: African American Images, 2002), pp. 97-98.
4. Tobias, Cynthia. *The Way We Learn* (Carol Stream: Tyndale, 1994), p. 19.
5. Armstrong, Thomas. *Multiple Intelligences* (Alexandria: ASCD, 2009), p. 33.
6. Dunn, Rita. *Differentiating Instruction* (Lanham: Rowman, 2009), p. 23.
7. Rapp, David. "The End of Textbooks? What's Stopping Districts from Ditching Paper Textbooks for Good?"
8. Chambers, Jay G., Thomas B. Parrish, and Jennifer J. Harr. *What We Are Spending on Special Education Services in the United States.* Special Education Expenditure Project, Center for Special Education Finance, 2004. http://csef.air.org/publications/seep/national/AdvRept1.pdf. See also: Raphael, Steven and Michael A. Stoll, eds. *Do Prisons Make Us Safe? The Benefits and Costs of the Prison Boom* (New York: Russell Sage Foundation, 2009), p. 280.
9. Moore, James L., Donna Y. Ford, and H. Richard Milner. "Underachievement among Gifted Students of Color," *Theory into Practice.* Spring 2005, p. 3.
10. Dunn, Rita. *Differentiating Instruction,* p. 12.

11. Gordon, Bennett. "For Art's Sake," *Utne Reader,* April 14, 2009. http://www.utne.com/Arts/For-Arts-Sake.aspx. See also: Zhan, Cindy. "The Correlation Between Music and Math: A Neurobiology Perspective," January 16, 2008. http://serendip.brynmawr.edu/exchange/node/1869.
12. Sax, Leonard. "Six Degrees of Separation: What Teachers Need to Know about the Emerging Science of Sex Differences," *Educational Horizons,* Spring 2006, pp. 190-200. http://www.boysadrift.com/ed_horizons_pdf.
13. Kunjufu, Jawanza. *Black Students, Middle-Class Teachers.* See also: Kunjufu, Jawanza. *100+ Educational Strategies* (Chicago: African American Images, 2008); Kunjufu, Jawanza. *200+ Educational Strategies* (Chicago: African American Images, 2009); and Lampi, Andrea, R., Nicole S. Fenty, and Cathrine Beaunae. "Making the Three Ps Easier: Praise, Proximity, and Precorrection," *Council for Children with Behavioral Disorders,* Fall 2005, pp. 8-12. http://www.ccbd.net/documents/bb/Fall2005 vol15no1pp8-12.pdf.
14. Owens, Judith, Katherine Belon, and Patricia Moss. "Impact of Delaying School Start Time on Adolescent Sleep, Mood, and Behavior," *Archives of Pediatrics & Adolescent Medicine,* July 2010. See also: Tharp, Bridget. "Harlem Start Time Change Part of School Movement," *Rockford Register Star,* December 16, 2007. http://www.rrstar.com/news/x805331439.
15. Cohen, Louis, Lawrence Manion, and Keith Morrison. *A Guide to Teaching Practice* (London: Psychology Press, 2004), p. 175.

Chapter 5: Peer Learning

1. Gifford-Smith, Mary, et al. "Peer Influence in Children and Adolescents: Crossing the Bridge from Developmental to Intervention Science," *Journal of Abnormal Child Psychology,* June 2005, pp. 255-265. http://www.ncbi.nlm.nih.gov/pmc/articles/PMC2747364/. See also: Gonzales, Nancy A., et al. "Family, Peer, and Neighborhood Influences on Academic Achievement among African-American Adolescents: One-Year Prospective Effects," *American Journal of Community Psychology,* Fall 1996, pp. 365-387.

2. Alvarado, Rafael. "Overcoming Fear of Gaming: A Strategy for Incorporating Games into Teaching and Learning," *Educause Quarterly,* vol. 3, no. 3, 2008, pp. 4-5. See also: Doshi, Ameet. "How Gaming Could Improve Information Literacy," *Computers in Libraries,* May 2006, pp. 14-17.
3. "KIPP: Knowledge Is Power Program," Making Schools Work, PBS.org. http://www.pbs.org/makingschoolswork/sbs/kipp/index.html.
4. Balfanz, Robert. "Can the American High School Become an Avenue of Advancement for All?" *America's High Schools,* Spring 2009. http://futureofchildren.org/futureofchildren/publications/journals/article/index.xml?journalid=30&articleid=35&sectionid=63. See also: Eagelson, Rebecca. "Higher Student Teacher Ratio May Lower Academic Achievement," *San Jose Examiner,* June 29, 2009. http://www.examiner.com/education-issues-in-san-jose/higher-student-teacher-ratios-may-lower-academic-achievement.
5. Conrad, Cecelia, ed., et al. *African Americans in the U.S. Economy* (Lanham: Rowman & Littlefield, 2005), p. 260.

Chapter 6: Gender Differences

1. Fletcher, Ralph J. *Boy Writers: Reclaiming Their Voices* (Portland: Stenhouse Publishers, 2006), pp. 71-80.
2. Fletcher, Ralph J. *Boy Writers,* p. 73.
3. *ibid.*
4. *ibid.*
5. Gurian, Michael. *Boys and Girls Learn Differently* (San Francisco: Jossey-Bass, 2001), pp. 20-26.
6. Wardle, Francis. "The Challenge of Boys in Our Early Childhood Programs," *Early Childhood News,* Fall 2000, pp. 4-12. http://www.earlychildhoodnews.com/earlychildhood/article_view.aspx?ArticleID=414.
7. Hale, Janice. *Learning While Black* (Baltimore: Johns Hopkins University Press, 2001), p. 118.
8. Kunjufu, Jawanza. *Countering the Conspiracy to Destroy Black Boys* (Chicago: African American Images, 1995 edition), pp. 18-19. See also: McGuinnes, Diane. *When Children Don't Learn: Understanding the Biology and Psychology of Learning Disabilities* (New York: Basic Books, 1986).

9. Tyre, Peg. "The Trouble with Boys," *Newsweek,* January 30, 2006. http://www.newsweek.com/2006/01/29/the-trouble-with-boys.html.

10. "Chicago Public Schools Flunk Black Students," *Chicago Reporter,* August 13, 2007. See also Elkind, David. *The Hurried Child,* p. 68.

11. King, Robert. "IPS Kids Repeat Kindergarten at a High Rate, But Does It Help?" IndyStar.com, October 10, 2010. http://www.indystar.com/article/201010100245/LOCAL/10100393.

12. "Attention Deficit Disorder (Short Attention Span)," Kids Growth.com. http://www.kidsgrowth.com/resources/articledetail.cfm?id=1007. See also: Coleman, Mary. "Serotonin Concentrations in Whole Blood of Hyperactive Children," *Journal of Pediatrics,* vol. 78, issue 6, June 1971, pp. 985-990.

13. Murphy, Patricia. *Equity in the Classroom* (New York: Routledge, 1996), pp. 5, 178-179.

14. Biederman, Joseph, et al. "The Longitudinal Course of Comorbid Oppositional Defiant Disorder in Girls with ADHD: Findings from a Controlled, Five-Year Prospective Longitudinal Follow-up Study," *Journal of Developmental Behavioral Pediatrics,* December 2008, pp. 501-507. See also: Cosentino, Barbra Williams. "ADHD: The Differences Between Boys and Girls," Kaboose.com. http://www.parenting.kaboose.com/education-and-learning/learning-disabilities/adad-and-differences-between-boys-and-girls.html.

15. Ferguson, Ann. *Bad Boys* (Ann Arbor: University of Michigan Press, 2001), pp. 86-87.

16. "Physical Education," *School Health Policies and Programs Study,* CDC 2006. http://www.cdc.gov/HealthyYouth/spps/2006/factsheets/pdf/FS_PhysicalEducationSHPPS2006.pdf.

17. Robert Wood Foundation. *Active Education,* Fall 2007.

18. Castelli, Darla M., et al. "Physical Fitness and Academic Achievement in Third- and Fifth-Grade Students," *Journal of Sport & Exercise Psychology,* vol. 29, 2007, pp. 239-252. See also: Grissom, James B. "The Relationship Between Physical Fitness and Academic Achievement," *Journal*

of Exercise Physiology, vol. 8, no. 1, 2005, pp. 11-25. http://asep/org/files/Grissom.pdf; Kim, Hye-Young, et al. "Academic Performance of Korean Children Is Associated with Dietary Behaviours and Physical Status," *Asia Pacific Journal of Clinical Nutrition,* vol. 12, no. 2, 2003, pp. 186-192.

19. "World University Rankings 2010-2011," Organization for Economic Cooperation and Development, September 2010. http://www.community. oced.org.

20. *ibid.*

21. "Physical Education, Physical Activity and Academic Performance," *Active Living Research,* Fall 2007. http://www.activelivingresearch.org/files/Active.Ed.pdf.

22. "Physical Education, Physical Activity and Academic Performance," *Active Living Research,* Summer 2009. http://www.rwjf.org/files/research/20090925a/ractive education.pdf.

23. *ibid.*

24. Coates, Julie and William A. Draves. "Smart Boys, Bad Grades," Learning Resources Network, 2006. http://www.smartboysbadgrades.com/smartboys_badgrades.pdf.

Chapter 8: Reading

1. O'Cummings, Mindee, Sarah Bardack, and Simon Gonsoulin. *The Importance of Literacy for Youth Involved in the Juvenile Justice System.* National Evaluation and Technical Assistance Center, January 2010. http://www. neglected-delinquent.org/nd/docs/literacy_brief_20100 120.pdf.

2. *ibid.*

3. *ibid.*

4. Elkind, David. *The Hurried Child,* p. 37.

5. Kunjufu, Jawanza. *An African Centered Response to Ruby Payne's Poverty Theory* (Chicago: African American Images, 2006); Kunjufu, Jawanza. *Reducing the Black Male Dropout Rate* (Chicago: African American Images, 2010). See also: Jimerson, Shane, et al. "Exploring the Association Between Grade Retention and Dropout," *California School Psychologist,* vol. 7, 2002, pp. 51-62. http://education.ucsb.edu/ jimerson/retention/CSP_RetentionDropout2002.pdf.

6. Garland, Sarah. "Repeat Performance," *The American Prospect,* October 25, 2010. http://www.prospect.org/cs/articles?article=repeat_performance. See also: Louise Kennelly and Maggie Monrad. *Approaches to Dropout Prevention: Heeding Early Warning Signs with Appropriate Interventions.* National High School Center, 2007. http://www.betterhighschools.org/docs/NHSC_Approachesto DropoutPrevention.pdf.

7. Orton-Gillingham Institute for Multi-Sensory Education, Northville, Michigan.http://www.orton-gillingham.com.

Chapter 9: Who Wants to Teach African American Males?

1. Kunjufu, Jawanza. "Black Boys and Special Education—Change Is Needed!"

2. "Men Struggling to Finish at Black Colleges," Associated Press, March 28, 2009, MSNBC.com. http://www.msnbc.com/id/29933480/ns/us_news-life.

3. Evans, A. L., et al. "Historically Black Colleges and Universities," *Education,* vol. 15, Fall 2002. http://findarticles.com/p/articles/mi_qa3673/is_1_123/ai_n28956838.

4. The Call Me MISTER Program, Clemson University. http://www.clemson.edu/hehd/departments/education/research-service/callmemister.

5. Billingsley, ReShonda Tate. "Black Male Teachers Key to Fixing National Crisis," *District Chronicles,* September 5, 2010. http://media.www.district chronicles.com/media/storage/paper263/news/2010/09/05/Cover/Black.Male. Teachers.Key.to.Fixing.National.Crisis-3927782.shtml.

6. Dee, Thomas S. "Teachers, Race and Student Achievement in a Randomized Experiment," National Bureau of Economics Research, Working Paper No. 8432, August 2001. http://www.nber.org/papers/w8432.

7. Kunjufu, Jawanza. *An African Centered Response to Ruby Payne's Poverty Theory.* See also: Darling-Hammond, Linda. "The Flat Earth and Education: How America's Commitment to Equity Will Determine Our Future," *Educational Researcher,* August/September 2007, pp. 318-334. http://www.aera.net/uploadedFiles/Publications/Journals/Educational_Researcher/3606/09edr07_318-334.pdf.

Chapter 10: Additional Solutions

1. For information on Robert Moses, founder of the Algebra Project in Cambridge, Massachusetts, see: http://www.algebra. org/staff.php. See also: Muhammad, Shahid. *How to Teach Math to Black Students* (Chicago: African American Images, 2002).
2. Kitsis, Aleksandr. "Benefits of Chess for Academic Performance and Creative Thinking," http://www.vivacityinc. com/chess/Articles/Benefits_ofChess.pdf.

Epilogue: The Ideal Black Male Classroom

1. Kunjufu, Jawanza. *Developing Positive Self-Images and Discipline in Black Children* (Chicago: African American Images, 1984).
2. Dunn, Rita. *What If,* p. 102.

Hey, it's FREDDDDD!!!!

Check out my new book of HACKIN' AWESOME school jokes! Homework excuses, jokes for the school lunchroom, monster report cards – s'all here. Plus tons of TOP TEN LISTS like SIGNS YOU'RE NOT A COMPUTER GEEK and WHAT TO SAY TO THE SCHOOL BULLY. Kevin, are u reading this?

You'll slurp up FRED'S GROSS-OUT SCHOOL CAFETERIA MENU, MY HANDY CLIP-AND-USE SCHOOL EXCUSES, and FRED'S SASSY ANSWERS TO SILLY QUESTIONS. Plus quizzes like HOW DUMB IS KEVIN? and TEST YOUR FRED I.Q.!

Wooooo! Hey, Judy!!! Check it OUT.

Peace out, home dawg!

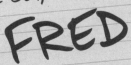

FRED

FRED'S TOP TEN
EXCUSES FOR BEING LATE TO SCHOOL

1 I had to walk the ferret.

2 The sign said, "School Ahead. Go Slow." So I did.

3 My dog ate my alarm clock.

4 Today, I rode on TOP of the bus.

5 I'm practicing to be The Invisible Man.

6 I had to match my socks to my underwear.

7 My watch is set to Shanghai time.

8 I told you if I wasn't there, you should start without me.

9 Had to help Batman catch the Joker.

10 I'm actually early for school – TOMORROW!

GETTING TO SCHOOL

These'll drive you crazzzzy!

WHY WAS THE COMPUTER LATE TO SCHOOL?

It had a hard drive.

WHAT PART OF A SCHOOL BUS IS THE MOST TIRED?

The exhaust pipe.

HOW DO BEES GET TO SCHOOL?

The school buzz.

HOW IS A SCHOOL BUS DRIVER DIFFERENT FROM A COLD?

One knows the stops, one stops the nose.

WHEN DO BUS DRIVERS STOP TO EAT?

When there's a fork in the road.

WHY WERE THE STRAWBERRIES LATE TO SCHOOL?

They were in a traffic jam.

WHAT DID THE FIRST STOPLIGHT SAY TO THE SECOND STOPLIGHT?

Don't look—I'm changing!

KNOCK KNOCK.

Who's there?

POLO.

Polo who?

POLO-VER, YOU'RE UNDER ARREST.

Why didn't Judy ride her bike to school?

Because it was two-tired.

WHY COULDN'T THE FROG FIND HIS CAR?

It was toad.

WHICH SNAKES ARE FOUND ON CARS?
Windshield vipers!

WHO CAN HOLD UP A SCHOOL BUS WITH ONE HAND?
A crossing guard.

KNOCK KNOCK.
Who's there?
RV.
RV who?
RV THERE YET?

KNOCK KNOCK.

Who's there?

MISTY.

Misty who?

MISTY BUS AGAIN, SO I HAVE TO WALK!

FRED'S TOP TEN

THINGS YOU DON'T WANT TO HEAR FROM THE BUS DRIVER

1 I'm on an all-beans diet.

2 You wouldn't believe how easy it is to get a driver's license!

3 Change the music? Sure, I have other polka CDs.

4 I've been accident-free for two whole weeks!

5 This is Sparky, my seeing-eye dog.

6 Want to see me pop a wheelie?

7 When the needle sinks below "E," what does that mean?

8 Does anyone have a spare tire?

9 Werewolf? No, I just forgot to shave my back hair.

10 Wheeeeeeeeeeeee!!!!!

CLASSY JOKES FROM FRED

Yo, everything's s'cool.

FRED: I FLUNKED CLASS. I FLUNKED CLASS

Judy: Why did you say that twice?

FRED: MY TEACHER SAID I HAD TO REPEAT THIS GRADE.

WHY WAS THE CLOCK PUNISHED?

Because it tocked too much.

WHAT TESTS DO THEY GIVE AT BEAUTY SCHOOL?

Make up exams.

WHY DID THE GIRL BRING SCISSORS TO SCHOOL?

She wanted to cut class.

9

TEACHER: *Sometimes I think you come to school just to cause trouble.*

FRED: *No, but as long as I'm here . . .*

WHY DO MAGICIANS MAKE GOOD TEACHERS?
They ask trick questions.

TEACHER: *If anyone has to go to the bathroom, hold up two fingers.*

FRED: *How will that help?*

WHY WAS THE TEACHER CROSS-EYED?
He couldn't control his pupils.

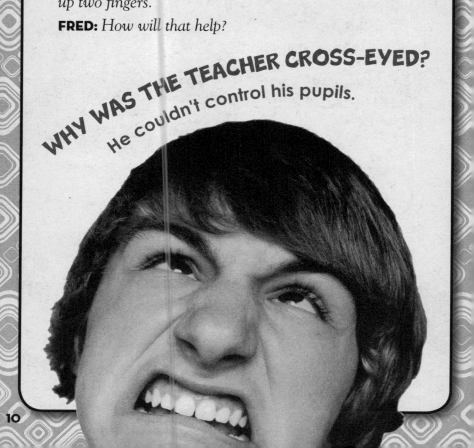

FRED'S TOP TEN

THINGS YOU'LL NEVER HEAR A TEACHER SAY

1 If you want my attention, scream!

2 Sorry, I didn't realize you were busy texting.

3 You'll never use algebra in real life.

4 If you don't practice on your DS, how will you get better?

5 Open your comic books to page 2.

6 Anyone mind if I take a nap?

7 When the bell rings, race to the door as fast as you can!

8 Outside voices, people.

9 Why don't you write your book report on Fred Figglehorn's Hackin' Awesome School Jokes?

10 Noise, please.

WHY DID THE TEACHER JUMP IN THE LAKE?

She wanted to test the waters.

KEVIN: *Give me all your money, or you're algebra!*
FRED: *You mean history?*
KEVIN: *Don't change the subject!*

WHY DID THE BOXER BRING HIS GLOVES TO THE LIBRARY?

His teacher said to hit the books.

TEACHER: *Please don't hum while you're working.*
FRED: *But I'm not working—I'm just humming.*

JUDY: *Want to go shopping today?*
FRED: *Can't. I have to help mom with my homework.*

WHAT HAPPENED WHEN THE TEACHER TIED HIS STUDENTS' SHOELACES TOGETHER?

They went on a class trip.

FRED: DO BOATS LIKE THE *TITANIC* SINK VERY OFTEN?

Teacher: Usually just once.

WHY DID THE BOY GLUE HIMSELF TO A BOOK?

The teacher said to stick to one subject.

HOW DID THE PEN KNOW IT WAS ABOUT TO BE THROWN OUT?

It had an ink-ling.

WHY DID THEY FLUNK?

THE LIGHT BULB?
It wasn't very bright.

THE MATH BOOK?
It had too many
problems.

THE CANNIBAL?
Tried to butter up
his teacher.

THE XEROX MACHINE?
It copied.

FRED FIGGLEHORN?
He had two F's.

THE DEAD SQUIRREL?
His grades were
rotten.

WHY DID KEVIN BRING A LADDER TO SCHOOL?

He wanted to go to high school.

HOW DOES A TEACHER SEND HIS PACKAGES?

First class.

TEACHER: *Can you name the Great Lakes?*

FRED: *They've already been named.*

FRED: WHY ARE YOU EATING YOUR EXAM?

KEVIN: The teacher said it was a piece of cake.

JUDY: *Did you know girls are smarter than boys?*
FRED: *No.*
JUDY: *See what I mean?*

HOW DO YOU GET STRAIGHT A'S?
With a ruler.

WHAT DO HISTORY TEACHERS TALK ABOUT WHEN THEY GET TOGETHER?
Old times.

WHY DID THE ASTRONAUT ORDER A PIZZA?
It was launch time.

FRED'S TOP TEN
NO-FAIL HOMEWORK EXCUSES

1 Someone broke into our house and stole my math book.

2 My mom used it as a baby wipe.

3 I was busy planning Teacher Appreciation Day.

4 Used it to polish the school statue.

5 Didn't want to add to your already heavy workload.

6 I gave it to you. Don't tell me you lost it!

7 The Giants were down a player and needed me.

8 My dog ate it, and another dog ate him.

9 Aliens made me promise not to tell.

10 Homework? We had homework?

WHY DID THE ALGEBRA TEACHER EXCUSE HERSELF?

She had to go to the mathroom.

WHY DID KEVIN BRING SOAP TO SCHOOL?

The weatherman predicted showers.

WHY DID THE MATH TEACHER CRY ON THE LAST DAY OF SCHOOL?

He hated to be divided from his class.

KNOCK KNOCK.

Who's there?

LOCKER.

Locker who?

LOCKER OUT, BUT LET ME IN!

KNOCK KNOCK.

Who's there?

PENCIL

Pencil who?

PENCIL FALL DOWN IF YOU DON'T WEAR A BELT!

KNOCK KNOCK.

Who's there?

TEACHER.

Teacher who?

TEACHER A LESSON SHE WON'T FORGET!

KNOCK KNOCK.

Who's there?

GRAMMAR.

Grammar who?

GRAMMAR'S A NICE OLD LADY!

KNOCK KNOCK.

Who's there?

OSCAR.

Oscar who?

OSCAR A STUPID QUESTION, GET A STUPID ANSWER!

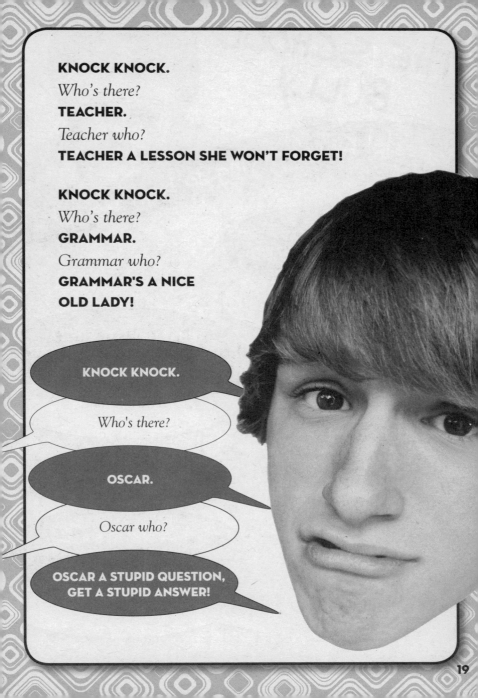

THE SCHOOL BULLY

Heeeelp! Kevin's trying to beat me up!

WHY DID THE BULLY TAKE OFF HIS WATCH?

Because time will tell.

WHAT TIME IS IT WHEN A GANG OF BULLIES CHASE YOU?

Five after one.

BULLY: GIVE ME A DOLLAR FOR A SANDWICH.

Fred: Okay, but it won't taste very good.

WHY DID THE BULLY GO TO THE BAKERY?

He heard the brownies were rich.

DID YOU HEAR ABOUT THE BULLY IN THE LAUNDROMAT?

He made a clean getaway.

HOW DID THE BARBER ESCAPE FROM THE BULLY?

He knew all the short cuts.

HOW DID THEY CATCH THE BULLY AT THE PIG FARM?

Someone squealed.

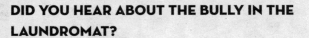

FRED'S TOP TEN
THINGS TO SAY TO THE SCHOOL BULLY

1 Sorry, my fight calendar's crazy busy.

2 Just name the place – Dad will drop me in his squad car.

3 Can't. I have to visit the last guy I sent to the hospital.

4 I'd love to, but I have karate class.

5 Have you met, Fangs, my pet snake?

6 I'm probably not contagious.

7 You know, I barf when I'm nervous.

8 Sorry, fighting is against my religion.

9 I can't until my leprosy clears up.

10 Mercy! Mercy!

THE SCHOOL CAFETERIA

Talk about TASTELESS!!!!

FRED: CAN I HAVE ANOTHER APPLE?

Cafeteria worker: No! Do you think they grow on trees?

HOW CAN YOU TELL IF A CLOCK IS HUNGRY?

It goes back for seconds.

WHAT DO YOU CALL CHEESE THAT'S NOT YOURS?

Nacho cheese.

WHY DID THE CAVEMAN SMASH HIS BREAD?

He wanted a clubbed sandwich.

WHY WAS THE WATER FOUNTAIN ARRESTED?

It was drunk in a public place.

WHERE DID THEY PUT THE LETTUCE THIEF?

Behind salad bars.

FRED'S TOP TEN

SIGNS YOU'VE HAD
A BAD SCHOOL LUNCH

1 The tastiest item is the Styrofoam cup.

2 HAZMAT guys take a sample of it.

3 It smells like tube socks.

4 Soup is served out of the janitor's bucket.

5 Two words: Horsemeat kebabs.

6 An ambulance is parked outside.

7 "Barely Soup" isn't a typo.

8 Your hamburger has a tail.

9 The cookies are green, and it's not St. Patrick's Day.

10 It's moving.

CAN EGGS MAKE THE HONOR ROLL?

Only if they're Grade A.

WHY DID THE GIRL TOSS A HAMBURGER AT HER FRIEND?

She wanted to throw him a surprise patty.

WHERE DO MATH TEACHERS EAT?

At the lunch counter.

IF A CARROT RACED A LETTUCE, WHO WOULD WIN?

The lettuce, because it's a head.

WHO'S THE LEADER OF THE POPCORN?

The kernel.

HOW DO SCHOOLS PREVENT CRIME IN THE LUNCHROOM?

With a burger alarm.

FRED'S GROSS-OUT SCHOOL

Cafeteria Menu

MONDAY

Tossed-cookie salad

Cream of washroom soup

Potatoes au Rotten

Mice pudding

TUESDAY

Spit pea soup

Sweat and sour chicken

Chocolate cow chip cookies

WEDNESDAY

Beef spew

Lice and beans

Hot sludge sundae

THURSDAY

Selection of old cuts

French flies

Green beings

Slime Jell-O

FRIDAY

Nixed salad

Tuna smelt

Tattered tots

Ice cream: Rocky Roadkill

THE SCHOOL CAFETERIA

KNOCK KNOCK.
Who's there?
PEAS.
Peas who?
PEAS TO MEET YA!

DID YOU HEAR ABOUT THE MAN WHO MARRIED HIS SILVERWARE?
Now they're man and knife.

WHY DID THE BIRD SING IN THE LUNCHROOM?
He got the urge to tweet.

WHAT FRUIT WILL NEVER RUN AWAY AND GET MARRIED?
A cantaloupe.

KNOCK KNOCK.

Who's there?

MUFFIN.

Muffin who?

MUFFIN VENTURED, MUFFIN GAINED.

KNOCK KNOCK.

Who's there?

OMELET.

Omelet who?

OMELET SMARTER THAN I LOOK!

KNOCK KNOCK.

Who's there?

OLIVE.

Olive who?

OLIVE THESE JOKES ARE TERRIBLE!

KNOCK KNOCK.

Who's there?

LETTUCE.

Lettuce who?

LETTUCE IN ALREADY!

JUDY: *Why are you staring at that orange juice box?*

FRED: *It says "concentrate."*

WHY DO FRENCH FRIES MAKE GOOD TV REPORTERS?

Because they're common taters.

HOW DO YOU MAKE...

A BANANA SPLIT?

Tell it to leave.

A STRAWBERRY SHAKE?

Make it nervous.

A FRUIT PUNCH?

Challenge it to a fight.

KNOCK KNOCK.
Who's there?
MISTER E.
Mister E. who?
MISTERY MEAT FOR LUNCH AGAIN!

Why was the mustard last in the race?
It couldn't ketchup.

What did the cook say to the salad?
"You're old enough to dress yourself."

Knock Knock.
Who's there?
Turnip
Turnip who?
Turnip the heat, I'm freezing!

HOW DO YOU FIX A BROKEN PIZZA?
With tomato paste.

MONSTERS IN SCHOOL

Yo! My babysitter's a vampire!

WHAT DO MUMMIES DO OVER SCHOOL VACATION?

Unwind.

HOW DO WITCHES LIKE THEIR BURGERS?

Medium scared.

WHY DID THE WITCH GET KICKED OUT OF CLASS?

She was hext-ing.

WHEN DID GODZILLA CROSS THE STREET?

When the sign said STALK.

HOW DOES A MONSTER COUNT TO 80?

On his fingers.

WHAT DOES THE BLOB SAY ON HIS VOICE MAIL?

"Leave a message at the sound of the creep."

WHAT DID THE TEACHER GIVE THE BLOB WHEN HE MISBEHAVED?

A slime-out.

WHO DID FRANKENSTEIN'S MONSTER TAKE TO THE PROM?

His ghoul friend.

WHY DO SKELETONS HATE RECESS?

They have no body to play with.

DID YOU HEAR ABOUT THE WITCHES' TALENT SHOW?

It was standing broom only.

WHAT JOB DO YOU GIVE THE SCHOOL WEREWOLF?

Howl monitor.

ZOMBIE #1: *How was the school dance?*
ZOMBIE #2: *Lousy. The place was dead.*

WHY DID THE GHOST GO TO THE NEWSSTAND?

He wanted chains for a dollar.

FRED'S TOP TEN

SIGNS YOUR TEACHER IS AN ALIEN

1 Urges you to try out for Martian band.

2 Fave candy: Milky Way.

3 Last place she taught was in the Freenus Quadrant.

4 Heats her burrito with a death ray.

5 Says, "Patience, people! I only have six hands!"

6 Drives a Mercury.

7 Spends time out of town . . . way out of town.

8 Has eyes in the back of her head – literally.

9 She ate the principal.

10 Thinks school cafeteria food is excellent.

IN THE CLASS PHOTO SHE'S THE ONE WITH THE TENTACLES!

37

WHY DID DRACULA RAISE HIS HAND?

He had to go to the bat room.

WHAT'S FRANKENSTEIN'S FAVORITE PART OF SCHOOL?

Making friends.

WHAT DID THE GHOST HAVE IN HIS ROCK COLLECTION?

Tombstones.

WHY DO WITCHES LIKE THE SCHOOL CAFETERIA?

They serve big potions.

WHY DID DRACULA GO TO THE SCHOOL NURSE?

Because of his coffin.

DID YOU HEAR ABOUT THE SCHOOL WITH A GHOST FOR A GROUNDS KEEPER?

He moans the lawn.

KNOCK KNOCK.
Who's there?
WEIRD
Weird who?
WEIRD I BE WITHOUT YOU?

KNOCK KNOCK.
Who's there?
WEREWOLF.
Werewolf who?
WEREWOLF I BE WITHOUT YOU?

KNOCK KNOCK.
Who's there?
HOWL.
Howl who?
HOWL I GET IN IF YOU DON'T OPEN UP?

KNOCK KNOCK

Who's there?

GOBLIN.

Goblin who?

GOBLIN MY LUNCH BEFORE IT ESCAPES!

WHAT DOES GODZILLA WATCH AT HOME?

A big-scream TV.

WHAT DOES GODZILLA EAT WHEN HE GOES TO THE SCHOOL CAFETERIA?

The school cafeteria.

REPORT CARDS FOR MONSTERS

THE GHOST

"Won't stay in his sheet."

THE HEADLESS HORSEMAN

"Incomplete."

THE INVISIBLE MAN

"Always absent."

HEY!!!! IF YOU KEPT YOUR MOUTHS SHUT, MAYBE YOU'D LEARN SOMETHING!

REPORT CARDS
FOR MONSTERS

THE ABOMINABLE SNOWMAN

"Freeze a jolly good fellow . . ."

DRACULA

"Has a bat attitude."

WITCH

"Flunking all her curses."

FRANKENSTEIN

"Borrows other students' brains and doesn't return them."

CYCLOPS

"One lousy pupil."

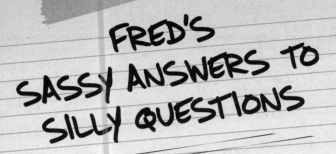

FRED'S SASSY ANSWERS TO SILLY QUESTIONS

KEVIN: Did you take the bus?
FRED: Why, is one missing?

SUBSTITUTE TEACHER: Are you chewing gum?
FRED: No, I'm Fred Figglehorn.

TEACHER: Why are you flying paper airplanes?
FRED: The big metal kind won't fit in my desk!

TEACHER: Can you pay attention?

FRED: I'm paying as little attention as possible.

TEACHER: Would you take out your math book?

FRED: I can't. I'm dating Judy!

TEACHER: Are you asleep?

FRED: No, I'm just using my head to hold the desk down.

TEACHER: Why did you miss school yesterday?

FRED: I didn't miss it at all!

MOM: How did you find school today?

FRED: I got off the bus, and there it was.

HI, TECH!

Homie G! These jokes are in hi-def.

WHERE DOES CYCLOPS BUY MUSIC ONLINE?

Eye-tunes.

HOW DO YOU PARK A COMPUTER?

Back it up.

WHY DID KEVIN BURY HIS CAMERA?

The battery was dead.

DID YOU HEAR ABOUT THE TRUCK THAT DELIVERED COMPUTERS?

It crashed.

MOTHER: I'D LIKE A WII FOR MY SON.

Clerk: We don't do trades.

WHY DID THE HUNGRY MAN BREAK OPEN HIS COMPUTER?

He heard there were chips inside.

WHY DID THE BASEBALL PLAYER SHUT DOWN HIS BLOG?

He wasn't getting any hits!

WHAT HAS A MONITOR, KEYBOARD, ANTENNAE, AND SIX LEGS?

A computer bug.

FRED'S TOP TEN

SIGNS YOU'RE NOT A
COMPUTER GEEK

1 You spray computer bugs with Raid.

2 You wear a helmet in case of a crash.

3 As far as you're concerned, a screensaver is a superhero.

4 When you see a menu, you order a hot dog.

5 You took Tylenol for a computer virus.

6 The screen is covered with Wite-Out.

7 To run a program, you take it jogging.

8 You put on galoshes to reboot.

9 You don't do Windows.

10 You're an adult.

WHY DID THE HACKER GO TO THE SCHOOL NURSE?

He had a bad code.

WHAT DID THE COMPUTER WRITE IN ITS OWNER'S YEARBOOK?

"Thanks for the memory."

WHERE DO TVS GO ON VACATION?

To remote places.

WHAT DO FROGS DO ON THE COMPUTER?

Wart processing.

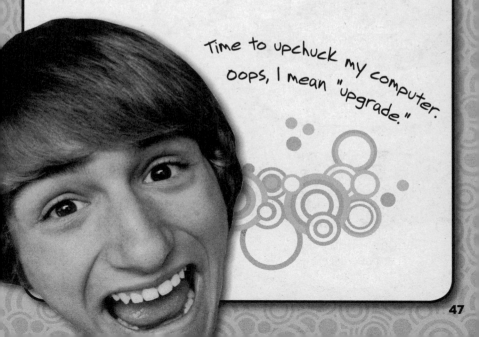

Time to upchuck my computer. Oops, I mean "upgrade."

THE SCHOOL NURSE

Woooo, these jokes are sick.

FRED: NURSE, I'M SHRINKING!

Nurse: Just be a little patient.

FRED: I KEEP HEARING A RINGING SOUND.

Nurse: Answer the phone!

WHAT DID ONE ELEVATOR SAY TO ANOTHER?

I think I'm coming down with something.

FRED: NURSE, NO ONE PAYS ATTENTION TO ME.

Nurse: Next!

WHEN DOES THE SCHOOL NURSE GET ANGRY?

When she runs out of patients!

NURSE: *Name?*

FRED: *Fred Figglehorn.*

NURSE: *Room?*

FRED: *216.*

NURSE: *Flu?*

FRED: *No, I walked. It's just around the corner.*

FRED: NURSE, SOMETIMES I THINK I'M MICKEY MOUSE

OTHER TIMES I THINK I'M DONALD DUCK!

Nurse: How long have you had these Disney spells?

FRED'S TOP TEN

THINGS THE SCHOOL NURSE IS TIRED OF HEARING

1 I'm allergic to algebra.

2 It was the Tofu Surprise.

3 I have Foosball Finger.

4 Faking it? How could I fake a 120° fever?

5 I have that two-hour flu that's going around.

6 It was the creamed cauliflower.

7 Do you get cartoons on that TV?

8 I have Video Game Elbow.

9 It was the chili squares.

10 Lice to meet you.

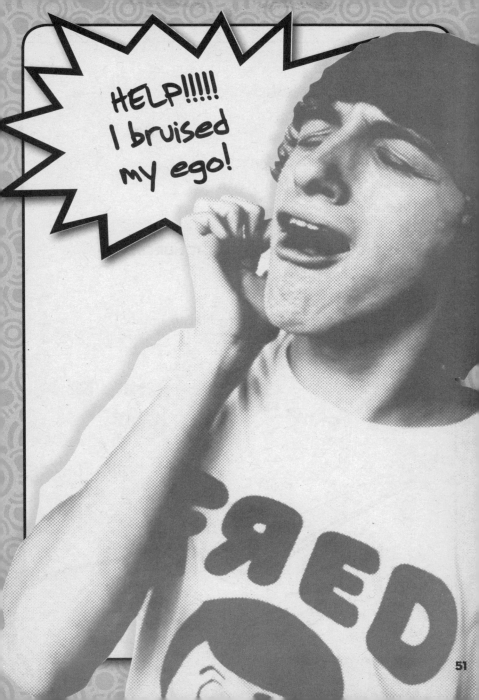

SCHOOL NURSE: *Try this bandage. You can play football, soccer, or basketball with it on.*
FRED: *Great! I couldn't do any of that before.*

FRED: *I have pimples all over my body!*
NURSE: *Is there anything else?*
FRED: *No, that zit.*

WHY DID THE CLOWN GO TO THE NURSE?
He was feeling funny.

FRED: *Nurse, the left side of my body is numb!*
NURSE: *You're all right.*

FRED: NURSE, I THINK I'M A GUITAR!

Nurse: You're just high strung.

FRED: *For the past few nights, I've snored so loudly, I've woken myself up. What should I do?*

NURSE: *Sleep in the next room!*

FRED: *Nurse, I swallowed my harmonica!*

NURSE: *Be glad you don't play the piano.*

FRED: NURSE, I FEEL LIKE A DECK OF CARDS.

Nurse: I'll deal with you later.

TEST YOUR FRED I.Q.

How well d'ya know me?

1. IN A SCHOOL PLAY, FRED PLAYED . . .

A. A TREE

C. VIDEO GAMES

B. SECOND CARROT ON THE LEFT

2. WHAT SCHOOL DID FRED GO TO?

A. BIBLE SCHOOL

C. SUNDAE SCHOOL

B. KNIGHT SCHOOL

3. FRED TRIED OUT FOR A DANCE GROUP CALLED

A. THE DISCO KIDS

C. NEW YORK CITY BALLET

B. THE FRISCO KIDS

4. WHAT DOES FRED LIKE ON HIS ICE CREAM?

A. PICKLES

C. BUTTER

B. MUSTARD

D. ALL OF THE ABOVE.

5. WHAT DOES FRED WANT TO BE WHEN HE GROWS UP?

A. A PEDIATRICIAN

C. TALLER THAN KEVIN

B. GROWN UP

6. WHAT DOES FRED THINK MAKES HIM POPULAR?

A. HE BRINGS STRAY ANIMALS TO SCHOOL

B. HE'S A GOOD SINGER

C. HE'S A GOOD DANCER

7. WHAT DID FRED WEAR TO THE SCHOOL DANCE?

A. HIS BEST KHAKIS WITH HIS ANKLES SHOWING

B. PULL-UPS

C. A WHITE DISCO SUIT

8. WHAT DID FRED DO ON HIS SNOW DAY?

A. MADE SNOW ANGELS

B. GOT BEAT UP BY KEVIN

C. BAKED COOKIES IN A DIRTY BOWL

D. ALL OF THE ABOVE

9. WHAT HAS FRED NOT BEEN KNOWN TO SAY?

A. HOUSTON, WE HAVE A PROBLEM

B. TALK TO THE HAND!

C. SHE NEEDS AN ATTITUDE CHECK

D. WANNA PLAY TWISTER?

SCORING:

IF YOU ANSWERED MOSTLY A AND D, YOU ARE A FRED GENIUS. IF YOU ANSWERED MOSTLY B OR C, YOU ARE A FRED ROOKIE (OR A GROWN-UP).

HOW DUMB IS KEVIN?

He's so dumb, he stole a free sample!!

He flunked lunch.

He thinks the English Channel is on basic cable.

He asked his barber to make his hair longer in the back.

He thinks Dr. Seuss makes house calls.

He had to cheat to get an F.

He thought The Hunchback of Notre Dame was about football.

He called himself EXIT to
see his name in lights.

He thinks an autobiography is a
car's life story.

He went to a garage sale to
buy a garage.

He went to the Gap to get
his teeth fixed.

He threw a rock at the
ground and missed.

He stayed up all night studying
for a blood test.

He tried to drown a fish.

FRED'S HANDY CLIP-AND-USE SCHOOL EXCUSES

✂ -

Dear Teacher,

Please excuse _____ from school for the next _____
             [your name]   [number]

days. He/she has a fever of a hundred and _____, and can't
                                    [high number]

keep down his/her _____. The doctor has diagnosed a rare
                    [candy]

strain of Mad _____ Disease. The only known cure is to
            [animal]

stay at home and play _____ until he/she reaches Level
                    [video game]

_____. He/she will be back to school soon, after watching
[number]

every episode of _____ at least_____times.
              [TV show]   [number]

Sincerely,

_____'s Mom
    [your name]

P.S. Please don't ever mention this note , because _____'s
                                       [your name]

illness is too upsetting. And don't call, because I'll be away in

_____ for the next _____ months, starting today.
[distant country]   [high number]

FRED'S TOP TEN

THINGS TO SAY WHEN YOU GET A BAD REPORT CARD

1 On the other hand, I'm doing great in lunch.

2 Isn't "D" for "delightful"?

3 The teacher discriminates against lazy kids.

4 That 60 in history refers to the class size.

5 I enjoyed the class so much I'm taking it again.

6 Told you I'm going down in history!

7 Four Ds and one C? Maybe I concentrated too much on one subject!

8 I thought it was like golf, where the lowest score wins.

9 After the holidays, everything gets marked down.

10 "C" you later!

SCHOOL'S OUT. YEAAAAAH!

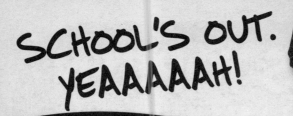

WHAT'S BETTER THAN VACATION?

More vacation!

WHY DID THE MOTHER PUT SUNBLOCK ON HER LITTLE BOY?

To prevent son burn.

WHY DID KEVIN TEAR A PAGE OUT OF HIS CALENDAR?

He wanted to take the month off.

WHAT DO YOU DO IF YOU'RE ADDICTED TO THE SUN?

Call a hotline.

WHAT KEEPS A SUMMER ROCK CONCERT COOL?

Thousands of fans!

WHY DID THE BEAR TIPTOE PAST THE CAMPSITE?

He didn't want to wake the sleeping bags.

DID YOU SEE THE NEW BEACH MOVIE?

It got wave reviews!

KNOCK-KNOCK.

Who's there?

SUMMER.

Summer who?

SUMMER FUNNY, SOME ARE NOT.

WHY DOES A DOG GET HOT IN THE SUMMER?

Because he has a coat and pants.

IT'S RHYME TO SAY GOODBYE

To a friend:
Roses are red, violets are blue,
I copied your paper, and I flunked too.

To Judy:
Someday you'll find out
What you missed
By never knowing
I exist

To your math teacher:
I know that you have often
Questioned my actions
But five out of four students
Have trouble with fractions.

To Kevin:
Hope you go someplace
Warm and sunny
Far away from
My lunch money

To someone you won't be seeing:
2 Busy
2 Get
2 Gether, so...
4 Get it!

To a teacher:
I know you like me
I know you care
But did you have to keep me
For a third straight year?

YOURS TILL . . .

. . . the ocean waves

. . . Niagara Falls

. . . the banana splits

. . . the board walks

. . . the bed spreads

. . . the kitchen sinks

. . . the chocolate chips

. . . the lettuce peeks to
see the salad dressing

. . . THE COCOA PUFFS

GOODBYE FROM FRED

Hey dawgs! One last joke for all my homies:

> **KNOCK KNOCK.**

> Who's there?

> **HACKIM.**

> Hackim who?

> **PRETTY HAKIM AWESOME!**

So long!

Ciao

Adios, Amigo

Smell ya later

CU L8TR

See ya, wouldn't wanna be ya!

Peace out

hasta La vista baby